450

W9-DBI-982

A Failure of Capitalism

A Failure of Capitalism

THE CRISIS OF '08 AND THE DESCENT INTO DEPRESSION

2009

Richard A. Posner

HARVARD UNIVERSITY PRESS

Cambridge, Massachusetts, and London, England

2009

Copyright © 2009 by the President and Fellows
of Harvard College

ALL RIGHTS RESERVED

PRINTED IN THE UNITED STATES OF AMERICA

Library of Congress Cataloging-in-Publication Data

Posner, Richard A.
   A failure of capitalism : the crisis of '08 and the descent into
depression / Richard A. Posner.
      p.   cm.
   Includes bibliographical references and index.
   ISBN 978-0-674-03514-0 (alk. paper)
     1. Financial crises—United States.   2. Depressions.
3. Capitalism.   4. United States—Economic conditions—2001–
5. United States—Economic policy—2001–   I. Title.
   HB3722.P67   2009
   330.973—dc22   2009004723

Contents

Preface

The world's banking system collapsed last fall, was placed on life support at a cost of some trillions of dollars, and remains comatose. We may be too close to the event to grasp its enormity. A vocabulary rich only in euphemisms calls what has happened to the economy a "recession." We are well beyond that. We are in the midst of the biggest economic crisis since the Great Depression of the 1930s. It *began* as a recession—that is true—in December 2007, though it was not *so* gentle a downturn that it should have taken almost a year for economists to agree that a recession had begun then. (Economists have become a lagging indicator of our economic troubles.) The recession had been triggered by a sharp nationwide drop in housing prices the previous summer that had caused the market in "subprime"—very risky—mortgage loans to collapse. Housing prices had been bid up

to unsustainable heights in the early 2000s. When
the market decided that houses were no longer
such a super investment, many people who were
overmortgaged relative to the value of their houses
defaulted, and either abandoned their house or
were forced out by foreclosure. The result was a
glut of unsold houses and a drastic reduction in the
amount of home building, as well as a great many
nonperforming mortgages. Two mortgage hedge
funds owned by the investment bank Bear Stearns
went broke in the summer of 2007, along with
American Home Mortgage Corporation and three
investment funds owned by the French bank BNP
Paribas. Countrywide Financial Corporation, the
nation's largest mortgage lender, narrowly averted
bankruptcy.

The recession was overtaken by a financial crisis
in March 2008, when Bear Stearns itself collapsed.
The crisis became acute in mid-September, when
the bankruptcy of Lehman Brothers, the distress
sale of Merrill Lynch, the near collapse and ensuing government takeover of Fannie Mae and
Freddie Mac (giant buyers and insurers of residential mortgages), and the bailout of American International Group, the nation's largest insurance
company, triggered a sharp drop in the stock mar-

ket and a worldwide credit freeze. Frantic efforts by the Federal Reserve, the Treasury Department, and Congress to save the financial system ensued. These efforts culminated in early October when Congress enacted a $700 billion bailout of the banking industry (TARP—the Troubled Asset Relief Program). But the bailout could not prevent the further deepening of the recession. By the end of 2008—with the Detroit automakers on the verge of bankruptcy and economic activity everywhere declining sharply, with the Dow Jones Industrial Average having declined to 8,800 (at this writing—February 2, 2009—it is down to 7,900) from 14,000 in October 2007 and from 11,100 as recently as September 26, and with the Federal Reserve making desperate efforts to prevent a deflation—the recession was beginning to be seen as the first U.S. depression since the Great Depression of the 1930s.

The word itself is taboo in respectable circles, reflecting a kind of magical thinking: if we don't call the economic crisis a "depression," it can't be one. But no one who has lived through the modest downturns in the American economy of recent decades could think them comparable to the present situation. The actions that the government has taken and plans to take bespeak fear that without radical measures of the kind that were or perhaps should have been taken during the Great Depression, we could find ourselves in almost as dire a predicament. It is the gravity of the economic downturn, the radicalism of the government's responses, and the pervading sense of crisis that mark what the economy is going through as a depression.

There is no widely agreed definition of the word, but I would define it as a steep reduction in output that causes or threatens to cause deflation and creates widespread public anxiety and, among the political and economic elites, a sense of crisis that evokes extremely costly efforts at remediation. It is too early to tell how protracted the downturn will be, and I recognize that protraction, so notable a feature of the Great Depression (especially in the United States), is a common marker for depressions. But it is expected to exceed in length every recession of the last half-century.

Not that we are likely to see a 34 percent drop in output or an unemployment rate of 24 percent, as in the depth of the Great Depression. But there is semantic space between a "Great Depression" and a mere recession, especially if, as may well happen in the present instance, a "successful" effort to avoid a repetition of the Great Depression will impose enormous long-term costs on the economy. The cost of a depression is not just the loss of output and employment before recovery begins; it is also the cost of the recovery, including such aftershock costs as inflation; there may be political costs as well.

At this writing, the federal government, in a desperate effort to speed the recovery, has spent or committed to spend (I include the stimulus package now wending its way through Congress, as it seems certain to be enacted) $7.2 trillion ($5.2 trillion by the Federal Reserve, $2 trillion by the Treasury Department), and has guaranteed another $2 trillion in loans and deposits. We are facing the certainty of a huge increase in the national debt and the possibility of a future inflation rate so high that, as in the early 1980s, the Federal Reserve will have to engineer a severe recession (by effecting a sudden sharp increase in interest rates) in order to restore price stability. Such a recession would be an aftershock, and hence a cost, of the present crisis. The aftershock would be all the greater if at the same time that interest rates were rising the government was raising taxes in order to trim an astronomical national debt. And suppose that to reduce the pain of a post-depression recession the Federal Reserve restarted the boom-and-bust cycle by forcing down interest rates. In short, even if the current downturn is arrested within months, the extraordinary measures that the government is taking to arrest it will cause profound economic problems for years.

Some conservatives believe that the depression is the result of unwise government policies. I believe it is a market failure. The government's myopia, passivity, and blunders played a critical role in *allowing* the recession to balloon into a depression, and so have several fortuitous factors. But without any government regulation of the financial industry, the economy would still, in all likelihood, be in a depression. We are learning from it that we need a more active and intelligent government to keep our model of a capitalist economy from running off the rails. The movement to deregulate the financial industry went too far by exaggerating the resilience—the self-healing powers—of laissez-faire capitalism.

To understand the economic crisis and draw the appropriate lessons while it is still unfolding will require our close attention to the following questions: What is this depression exactly—a mere li-

quidity crisis? a solvency crisis? something else?—
and what precipitated it? What are the underlying
causes? Why was it not anticipated? How well is
the government responding to it? Is the depression
unalloyed grief, or may it have some redemptive
political or economic consequences—the silver
lining that every self-respecting cloud should have?
What can we learn from it about capitalism, government, and the economics profession? What can
be done to head off future depressions? What individuals or institutions are most culpable for having
failed to foresee and avert the depression? What is
its principal political lesson? I organize my discussion around these questions.

The media's coverage of the crisis has been ex-
tensive, lively, often insightful, and even riveting,
though now it's turning silly, with ignorant denun-
ciations of "Wall Street" for greed and extravagance. (What did reporters think businessmen
were like?) The sheer volume of that coverage is
daunting, however, and much of it is anecdotal,
ephemeral, or both. There are books and articles
galore, both journalistic and academic, about depressions in general and even about this depression. But many of the writings are by authors with
an axe to grind, or are too technical for nonspecial-

ists to understand, or are months behind the curve, or assume too much prior knowledge of the financial system (are too "insiderish"), or, at the other extreme, are superficial. There is a need for a concise, constructive, jargon- and acronym-free, nontechnical, unsensational, light-on-anecdote, analytical examination of the major facets of the biggest U.S. economic disaster in my lifetime and that of most people living today. That is the need this book tries to fill.

My focus is on the course, causes, and offered cures of the depression. But I also emphasize some points that have received relatively little coverage in other accounts: the depression's political dimensions, the disappointing performance of the economics profession in regard to anticipating and providing guidance to responding to the depression, how ideology can distort economic policy, the inherent limitations of depression economics, how the self-interested decisions of rational businessmen and consumers can give rise to a depression (so there is no need to look for psychological explanations), and how the failure of officials and economists to anticipate the financial crisis and prevent its ripening into a depression echoes the failures of other officials and other professionals to anticipate and prevent other catastrophic events, like the Pearl Harbor or 9/11 attacks or the devastation of New Orleans by Hurricane Katrina. (In discussing these analogies I shall be drawing on my previous work on catastrophe and on intelligence failures. See my books *Catastrophe: Risk and Response* [2004] and *Preventing Surprise Attacks: Intelligence Reform in the Wake of 9/11* [2005].)

I have tried to be simple without being simplistic—to write for generalists but also to suggest points that may interest specialists. I have eschewed the usual scholarly apparatus of footnotes and citations, though I list some further readings at the end of the book for those who want to read more widely in a fascinating and timely subject. I have been assiduous in suppressing extraneous detail; the book is a high-altitude survey and, since I am not a macroeconomist, reflects an outsider's perspective—but there can be value in such a perspective.

By way of simplification, I do not distinguish between the overlapping governing bodies of the Federal Reserve System—the Board of Governors of the Federal Reserve System and the Federal Open Market Committee—but treat them as a single entity, the Federal Reserve. It is the Open Market

Committee rather than the board that controls the supply of money, but the same person is chairman of both and dominates both, so for my purposes there is no need to distinguish between the two bodies. I also use the words "bank" and "banking" broadly, to encompass all financial intermediaries (firms whose business is to lend borrowed capital), because the lines that used to separate commercial banks from investment banks and other nonbank financial intermediaries have so blurred. When I want to speak about banks in a narrow sense, but the context does not indicate that, I use the term "commercial bank."

The first five chapters describe how and why the economy has gotten itself into such a fix and what the government is trying to do to get the economy out of it and how likely it is to succeed. The last six chapters focus primarily on the lessons that can be learned from the debacle and from the efforts to avoid or mitigate it—lessons that may help us avoid the next depression.

Some might think it premature to write about a depression before it ends and indeed before it has reached bottom. But when it ends, hindsight will rewrite history. With the passage of the American Recovery and Reinvestment Act of 2009, expected within weeks, virtually all the imaginable weapons that can be used against a depression will have been deployed (though innumerable changes of course and emphasis can be expected), and it may take years to determine their efficacy and to experience any aftershocks of the depression, such as runaway inflation. This is a good juncture at which to take stock, albeit tentatively, preliminarily, of a momentous economic event that is likely to affect America and the world in profound ways. Irving Fisher's pathbreaking essay on the Great Depression appeared in 1933, long before that depression ended, and John Maynard Keynes's immensely influential *General Theory of Employment, Interest and Money* appeared in 1936, before the depression ended in the United States.

But because I am writing *in medias res*, I have decided to create a blog (I will call it "The Posner Economic Crisis Blog") in which I will blog weekly on the crisis, beginning a week after the publication of this book, in effect continuously updating the book. Comments from readers will be welcomed and posted, and I will respond to as many of the most insightful or informative comments as my time permits.

This will not be an entirely new venture for me.

The economist Gary Becker and I blog weekly on issues of economic policy. (See "The Becker-Posner Blog," http://becker-posner-blog.com/.) We began blogging about the nascent crisis back in June of 2007; and while I did not then foresee a depression, I expressed concerns that events have shown were realistic. Anyone interested in my thinking before I realized we were headed for a depression should look up my blog entries of June 24, August 19, and December 23, 2007. I have incorporated here and there in the book some materials from my blog entries beginning in September 2008, when the financial crisis hit with full force.

I thank my co-blogger, Gary Becker, for fruitful discussions of a number of the issues that I cover in the book, and Laura Bishop, Ralph Dado, Justin Ellis, Anthony Henke, and Michael Thorpe for their very helpful research assistance. I gained valuable insights from a talk by Robert Lucas and from helpful materials that he furnished me, and from a discussion with Lynn Maddox and an e-mail exchange with Myron Scholes. Lee Lockwood and Christian Opp carefully checked the manuscript for technical economic errors and in the process made valuable suggestions for improving the book. Michael Aronson, Douglas Baird,

Larry Bernstein, Michael Boudin, Nathan Christensen, Kenneth Dam, Benjamin Friedman, Rebecca Haw, Ashley Keller, William Landes, Jonathan Lewinsohn, Jennifer Nou, Charlene Posner, Eric Posner, Kenneth Posner, Raghuram Rajan, Andrew Rosenfield, Andrei Shleifer, and Luigi Zingales gave me extremely helpful comments on a previous draft. Friedman's help with my project deserves a special acknowledgment. I also owe special thanks to Aronson, my editor at the Harvard University Press, for his encouragement and deft management of this project, as well as for many insightful comments. None of the above is responsible for the errors that remain.

February 2, 2009

A Failure of Capitalism

I

The Depression and Its Proximate Causes

A SEQUENCE of dramatic events has culminated in the present economic emergency: low interest rates, a housing bubble, the collapse of the bubble, the collapse of the banking system, frenzied efforts at resuscitation, a drop in output and employment, signs of deflation, an ambitious program of recovery. I need to trace the sequence and explain how each stage developed out of the preceding one. This chapter opens with a brief sketch of the basic economics of depression and of fighting depression and then turns to the particulars of this depression.

Suppose some shock to the economy—say, a sudden fall in the value of people's houses and securities—reduces the value of personal savings and induces people to spend less so they can rebuild their savings. The demand for goods and services will therefore fall. Before the shock, demand and supply were both X; now demand is X − Y. How will suppliers respond? If—a critical assumption—all prices, including the price of labor (wages), are completely flexible, suppliers, including suppliers of labor—workers—will reduce their prices in an effort to retain as many buyers as possible. With consumers saving more because they are buying less, and at lower prices, interest rates—earnings on savings—will fall because there will be a savings glut. The lower interest rates will induce borrowing; and with more borrowing and lower prices, spending will soon find its way back to where it was before the shock. One reason this will happen is that not all consumers are workers, and those who are not, and whose incomes therefore are unimpaired, will buy more goods and services as prices fall.

The flaw in this classical economic theory of the self-correcting business cycle is that not all prices are flexible; wages especially are not. This is not primarily because of union-negotiated or other employment contracts. Few private-sector employers in the United States are unionized, and few non-unionized workers have a wage guaranteed by contract. But even when wages are flexible, employers generally prefer, when demand for their product drops, laying off workers to reducing wages. Think of all the financial executives who have been laid off even while bonuses—often amounting to half the executive's pay—were being cut, sometimes to zero.

There are several reasons that employers prefer layoffs to cutting wages. (1) Layoffs reduce overhead expenses. (2) By picking the least productive workers to lay off, an employer can increase the productivity of its workforce. (3) Workers may respond to a reduction in their wages by working less hard, or, conversely, may work harder if they think that by doing so they may reduce the likelihood that *they* will be laid off. (4) When the wages of all workers in a plant or office are cut, all are unhappy; with layoffs, the unhappy workers are off the premises.

If wages fall far enough, many workers will lay themselves off, finding better uses of their time (such as getting more schooling) than working for a pittance—and they may be workers whom the employer would have preferred to retain.

The reasons for employers' preference for layoffs are attenuated when instead of a worker's wage being cut he is reduced from full-time to part-time status. He is still part of the team; and he may be able to assuage his distress at his lower wage by adding another part-time job and thus restoring his full income. So reductions from full-time to part-time employment are more common than wage cuts. Similarly, a reduction in bonus is less demoralizing than a cut in salary. There is less expectation of receiving a bonus than of continuing to receive one's base salary, and so there is less disappointment when the bonus is cut.

When, in order to reduce output from X to X − Y in my example and thus restore equilibrium, producers and other sellers of goods and services, such as retailers, begin laying off workers, demand is likely to sink even further; that is, Y will be a larger number. Unemployment reduces the incomes of the formerly employed and creates uncertainty about economic prospects—the uncertainty of the unemployed about whether and when they will find comparable employment, the uncertainty of the still-employed about whether they will retain their jobs. Workers who are laid off spend less money because they have less to spend, and those not laid off fear they may be next and so begin to save more of their income. The less savings, especially safe savings, people have, the more they will reduce their personal consumption expenditures in order to increase their savings, and therefore the more that output will fall. Interest rates will fall too, but many people will be afraid to borrow (which would increase economic activity by giving them more money to spend). So spending will not increase significantly even though low interest rates reduce the cost of consumption; people will want to have precautionary savings because of the risk that their incomes will continue to decline.

Still, the downward spiral is unlikely to become uncontrollable even without radical government intervention unless the shocks that started the economy on the path to depression either were extremely severe or, because of widespread over-indebtedness, created default cascades that reduced banks' capital to a point at which they could no longer lend money in quantity. For then consumers who wanted to borrow to maintain their level of consumption could not do so, and their inability to borrow would accelerate the fall in demand for goods and services. Commercial activity would fall dramatically; it depends vitally on credit, in part just because costs of production and distribution are almost always incurred before revenues are received.

With demand continuing to fall, sellers lay off more workers, which exerts still more downward pressure on demand. They also reduce prices in an effort to avoid losing all their customers and be stuck with unsalable inventory. As prices fall, consumers may start hoarding their money in the expectation that prices will keep falling. And they will not borrow at all. For with prices expected to keep falling, they would be paying back their loans in dollars of greater purchasing power because the same number of dollars will buy more goods and services. That is deflation—money is worth more—as distinct from inflation, in which money is worth less because more money is chasing the same quantity of goods and services.

With demand continuing to fall, bankruptcies soar, layoffs increase, incomes fall, prices fall further, and so there are more bankruptcies, etc.—the downward spiral continues. Adverse feedback loops—"vicious cycles" in an older vocabulary—are a formula for catastrophe; other examples are pandemics and global warming. Irving Fisher, writing in the depths of the Great Depression, said that a depression was "somewhat like the 'capsizing' of a ship which, under ordinary conditions, is always near stable equilibrium but which, after being tipped beyond a certain angle, has no longer this tendency to return to equilibrium, but, instead, a tendency to depart further from it."

So it is not really the initial shock to a robust system that is the main culprit in a depression; it is the vulnerability of the process by which the system adjusts to a shock. This makes the adequacy of the institutional response to that vulnerability critical.

One institutional response to a deflationary spiral is for the Federal Reserve to increase the supply of money, so that a given number of dollars doesn't buy more goods than it used to. The Federal Reserve creates money in various ways. The most common one, but not the most intuitive, is by altering the federal funds rate; I discuss that later. Another way is by buying federal securities, such as T bills (T for Treasury), from banks. The cash the banks receive from the sale is available to them to lend, and loan proceeds, deposited in the borrower's bank account, increase the number of dollars available to be spent. Fearing deflation, the Federal Reserve has been expanding the money supply in the current crisis, but with limited success. Because banks are on the edge, or even over the edge, of being insolvent, they are fearful of making risky loans, as most loans in a depression are. So they have put more and more of their capital into short-term securities issued by the federal government—securities that, being backed by the full faith and credit of the United States, are safe.

The effect of competition to buy these securities has been to bid down the interest rate on them virtually to zero. Short-term federal securities that pay no interest are the equivalent of cash. When banks want to hold cash or its equivalent rather than lend it, the action of the Federal Reserve in buying cash-equivalent securities does nothing to increase the money supply. So the Fed is now buying other debt, and from other financial firms as well as from banks—debt that has a positive interest rate, the hope being that if the Federal Reserve buys the debt for cash the seller will lend out the cash in order to replace the interest income that it had been receiving on the debt. But this program has not yet had a great deal of success either. If people and firms are extremely nervous about what the future holds for them, low interest rates will not induce them to borrow.

If monetary policy does not succeed in equating demand to supply by closing the gap between demand of $X - Y$ and supply of X, maybe government spending can do the trick. The government can buy Y worth of goods and services, thus replacing private with public demand, or it can reduce taxes by Y (or give people after-tax income in some other form, such as increased unemployment benefits), so that people have more money to spend, or it can do some of both. Whichever course it follows, it will be engaged in deficit spending. The buying part of the program, like the tax cuts, can be financed only by borrowing (or by the Federal Reserve's creating money to pay for the program) and not by taxing, for if financed by taxation it would not increase aggregate demand; it would inject money into the economy with one hand and remove it with the other. (It was always obvious that the government could reduce unemployment by hiring people; what makes it a device for fighting a depression is doing so without financing the program by means of taxes.) At this writing, Congress is on the verge of enacting a massive deficit-spending program involving public spending on infrastructure improvement and other public-works-type projects, plus tax cuts and other subsidies.

Such is the anatomy of depression, and of recovery from depression. But there are different types of depression or recession and we must distinguish among them. In the least interesting and usually the least serious, some unanticipated shock, external to the ordinary workings of the market, disrupts the market equilibrium. The oil-price surges of the early and then the late 1970s, and the terrorist attacks of September 11, 2001 (which deepened a recession that had begun earlier that year), are illustrative. The second type, illustrated by the recession of the early 1980s, in which unemployment exceeded 10 percent for a part of 1982, is the induced recession. The Federal Reserve broke what was becoming a chronic high rate of inflation by a steep increase in interest rates. In neither type of recession is anyone at fault, and the second was beneficial to the long-term health of the economy.

The third and most dangerous type of recession/depression is caused by the bursting of an investment bubble. It is depression from within, as it were, and is illustrated by both the depression of the 1930s and the current one, though by other depressions and recessions as well, including the global recession of the early 1990s. A bubble is a steep rise in the value of some class of assets that cannot be explained by a change in any of the economic fundamentals that determine value, such as increased demand due to growth in population or to improvements in product quality. But often a bubble is generated by a *belief* that turns out to be mistaken that fundamentals *are* changing—that a market, or maybe the entire economy, is entering a new era of growth, for example because of technological advances. Indeed that is probably the main cause of bubbles.

A stock market bubble developed in the 1920s, powered by plausible optimism (the years 1924 to 1929 were ones of unprecedented economic growth) and enabled by the willingness of banks to lend on very generous terms to people who wanted to play the stock market. You had to put up only 10 percent of the purchase price of the stock; the bank would lend the rest. That was risky lending, since stock prices could and did decline by more than 10 percent, and explains why the bursting of the stock market bubble in 1929 precipitated widespread bank insolvencies. New profit opportunities and low interest rates had led to overindebtedness, an investment bubble, a freezing of credit when the bubble burst because the sudden and steep fall in asset prices caused a cascade of defaults, a rapid decline in consumption because people could not borrow, and finally deflation. Overindebtedness leading to deflation was the core of Irving Fisher's theory of the Great Depression, and there is concern that history may be repeating itself.

The *severity* of the 1930s depression may have been due to the Federal Reserve's failure to expand the supply of money in order to prevent deflation, a failure connected to our adherence to the gold standard: a country that allows its currency to be exchanged for a fixed amount of gold on demand cannot increase its money supply without increasing its gold reserves, which is difficult to do. The United States went off the gold standard in 1933, and there was an immediate economic upturn. Yet the depression persisted until the United States began rearming in earnest shortly before it entered World War II; its persistence may have been due to the Roosevelt Administration's premature abandonment of deficit spending, employed at the outset of the Administration along with the abandonment of the gold standard with apparent success in arresting the economic downturn.

There was a smaller bubble, in stocks of dotcom, telecommunications, and other high-tech companies, in the late 1990s. But its bursting had only a modest adverse effect on the economy as a whole, as did the sharp drop in the stock market triggered by the terrorist attacks of September 11, 2001.

The current economic emergency is similarly the outgrowth of the bursting of an investment bubble. The bubble started in housing but eventually engulfed the financial industry. Low interest rates, aggressive and imaginative marketing of home mortgages, auto loans, and credit cards, diminishing regulation of the banking industry, and perhaps the rise of a speculative culture—an increased appetite for risk, illustrated by a decline in the traditional equity premium (the margin by which the average return on an investment in stocks exceeds that of an investment in bonds, which are less risky than stocks)—spurred speculative lending, especially on residential real estate, which is bought mainly with debt. As in 1929, the eventual bursting of the bubble endangered the solvency of banks and other financial institutions. Residential-mortgage debt is huge ($11 trillion by the end of 2006), and many defaults were expected as a result of the bubble's collapse. The financial system had too much risk in its capital structure to take these defaults in stride. The resulting credit crisis—a drastic reduction in borrowing and lending, indeed a virtual cessation of credit trans-

actions, for long enough to disrupt the credit economy seriously—precipitated a general economic
downturn. The downturn depressed stock prices,
which exacerbated the downturn by making people feel poorer; for when they feel poorer, even before they become poorer, they spend less, as a precaution.

As the downturn deepened, bank solvency received a second shock: the default rate on bank
loans secured by assets other than residential real
estate rose because many borrowers were in financial straits. It is expected to rise further. The financial industry is beginning to resemble an onion:
one peels successive layers of debt and wonders
whether there is any solid core at all.

How severe is the economic downturn, and how
much worse is it likely to get? If one looks only at
statistics for 2008 (as we are still in the first quarter
of 2009), the situation does not look too terrible: an
unemployment rate of 7.2 percent and a gross domestic product (the market value of the nation's total output of goods and services) that in the last
three months of 2008 was 3.8 percent below its
level in the corresponding period the previous year.
But these snapshots of the economy are incomplete; there is also an $8 trillion decline in the

value of traded stocks since 2007 to be reckoned with, together with an estimated $2 trillion of losses by American banks. The snapshots are also misleading. At the beginning of 2008, the unemployment rate was below 5 percent, and few observers think that it has plateaued at 7.2 percent. And when discouraged workers and workers involuntarily working part-time rather than full-time are added to the "officially" unemployed, we discover that the percentage of underutilized workers increased from 8.7 percent in December 2007 to 13.5 percent a year later, implying a significant drop in income available to buy goods and services. The 3.8 percent decline in gross domestic product is also misleading, because the figure is likely to grow and because it would have been 5.1 percent had production for inventory been excluded. The buildup of inventory was the unintended result of an unanticipated fall in demand. Carrying charges for inventory are considerable, and the built-up inventories are likely to be liquidated at very steep discounts, which by pulling down the price level will increase the danger of a deflation. Until they are liquidated, moreover, production will be depressed, since sales from inventory are substitutes for sales of newly produced goods.

The distinguished macroeconomist Robert Lucas estimates that in 2008 the gross domestic product was 4.1 percent below where it would have been in an average year (that is, 4.1 percent below the long-term trend line of gross domestic product, which is upward), and that if one may judge from consensus forecasts of economic activity it will be 8.3 percent below the trend line in 2009. That is nothing to write home about if your benchmark is 1933 (34 percent), but it is greater than in any year since the end of the Great Depression. Another ominous sign is that almost every estimate of the economic situation has later been revised downward, which feeds pessimism both directly and by revealing that financial experts have an imperfect grasp of the situation; if they don't know what's happening, they're unlikely to be able to provide much guidance to arresting the downward spiral of the economy.

Personal consumption expenditures and consumer prices are falling significantly, which is uncharacteristic of mere recessions and is worrisome because deflation can greatly darken the economic picture. The consumer price index (seasonally adjusted) stopped rising in September 2008 and then fell 1.0 percent in October, 1.7 percent in November, and .7 percent in December. Another symptom of deflation is that many employers are cutting wages as well as laying off workers. This is an unusual response to economic adversity but makes sense in a deflation, when the purchasing power of money increases because prices are falling. For then a reduction in nominal wages need not mean a reduction in purchasing power (real wages). Indeed, unless nominal wages are cut in a deflation workers will be receiving higher wages in real terms—and for an employer to pay his workers more in an economic downturn would be anomalous.

What is important is not the price declines for the last three months of 2008 as such but whether they will engender expectations of further declines. If so, as we shall see in chapter 5, the result is likely to be hoarding of cash on a large scale, which would dry up economic activity. If one averages the declines in the consumer price index for the last three months of 2008 and projects them out for a year, the result is a more than 12 percent decline in consumer prices. That would be catastrophic. I am not predicting such a decline; I make no forecasts. But only deflation anxiety can explain the extraordinary efforts that the Federal Reserve has been making to increase the supply of money. The fact that the entire world has been caught up in our financial crisis is a further danger sign, because it foreshadows an economically disruptive reduction in foreign trade.

Still another portent is that it is a financial crisis rather than some other shock that is convulsing the economy. A similar financial crisis ushered in the deflationary stage of the Great Depression. The reason a financial crisis is such a downer is that the usual means by which the Federal Reserve pulls the economy out of a recession is by expanding the supply of money so that interest rates fall, which stimulates borrowing and hence, because most borrowing is for spending, whether on consumption or production, economic output. But the Federal Reserve does its money creation through the banks, and if the banks have solvency problems that make them reluctant to lend, the Fed's efforts to expand the money supply are impeded.

To understand the central role of the banks' problems in our economic plight, we need to understand the contemporary meaning of "bank" and how that meaning was produced by the movement to deregulate the financial industry. The genus of which "bank" is one of the species is "financial in-termediaries"—firms that borrow money and then lend (or otherwise invest, but my focus will be on lending) the borrowed money. The difference be-tween the cost of the borrowed money to the firm and the price it charges when it lends out the money that it has borrowed covers the firm's other costs and generates a profit. There are many differ-ent types of financial intermediary—commercial banks, trust companies, home-loan banks ("thrifts"), custodian banks, investment banks and other secu-rity broker-dealers, money market funds, other mutual funds, hedge funds, private equity funds, insurance companies, credit unions, and mortgage lenders (in the 1940s and 1950s my father had a suc-cessful business of making second-mortgage loans on commercial properties). But today the regula-tory barriers separating the different types of finan-cial intermediary have eroded to the point where, for most of my purposes in this book, all financial intermediaries can be regarded as "banks," even when different types of bank are combined in one enterprise—and that has become common too.

There isn't that much difference anymore even between a commercial bank and a hedge fund. Not that there is no difference. Commercial banks tend, paradoxically, to have riskier capital structures than hedge funds, in part because they have less equity capital and make longer-term loans and in part because some of their capital (demand deposits—the money in checking accounts) is federally insured. Commercial banks differ from all other financial intermediaries in only a few ways that remain important. The most important is their role, which I will be touching on from time to time, in expanding and contracting the supply of money in the U.S. economy.

We need to consider why—the answer is not obvious—the bursting of a housing bubble should cause banks to go broke. Long-term lending secured by mortgages on residential real estate has traditionally been thought a low-risk business activity. If the homeowner defaulted, the lender would (in effect) seize and sell the house. If real estate prices had fallen, the house might not be worth the unpaid principal of the mortgage, but this risk was minimized by the unwillingness of mortgagees (the lenders—the borrowers are mortgagors) to lend the entire purchase price of a house, or its entire market value if the house had been acquired earlier. The mortgagee would usually require the mortgagor to make a 20 percent down payment on the purchase, so that the mortgagee would be safe as long as the house did not lose more than 20 percent of its value.

Even then the loan might be pretty safe, because banks refused to make mortgage loans to people who would be likely, because of inadequate income, heavy debts, or other serious underwriting risks, to default on a loan. Discipline in lending was reinforced by state usury laws that are now largely preempted by federal law as a result of the deregulation movement. By limiting the interest rate that an individual could be charged, usury laws discourage the making of risky loans because the lender is forbidden to charge an interest rate high enough to compensate him for a high risk that the borrower will default.

We should consider why a lender would *want* to make a risky loan. The basic reason is that the greater the risk, the higher the interest rate, to compensate the lender for the possibility that the borrower will default and as a result the lender will not be repaid unless there is adequate collateral for the loan or the loan has been guaranteed by someone of substance. If the lender is able somehow to reduce or offset the risk, or just is lucky, or doesn't worry about the risk because it is likely to materialize, if at all, beyond his planning horizon, the risky loan will be more profitable than a safe loan would be. But before deregulation, banks would get into serious trouble with their regulators if they made risky loans, or at least enough risky loans to create a nontrivial risk of bankruptcy.

So there was safe lending, by banks, and risky lending by other financial intermediaries. One thing that made banks safe was that they were forbidden to pay interest on demand deposits, traditionally their major source of capital. Another was that they were required to hold a portion of their deposits in the form of cash or an account with a federal reserve bank. These assets constituted the bank's "reserves" and did not pay interest. They were riskless and so reduced the overall riskiness of the bank's asset portfolio. But then business depositors took to practicing "sweeps"—moving the money in their bank accounts into investment funds until they needed it to pay bills, at which point they moved it back. And money market funds arose to provide people with checkable accounts, just like bank accounts (though uninsured)—except that they paid interest. Banks responded by supplementing deposits as a source of bank capital with loans from other sources, on which they had to pay interest—

and hence had to lend their capital out at a higher interest rate than they were paying for the capital furnished by their depositors. This required them to make riskier loans. The deregulatory strategy of allowing nonbank financial intermediaries to provide services virtually indistinguishable from those of banks, such as the interest-bearing checkable accounts offered by money market funds, led inexorably to a complementary deregulatory strategy of freeing banks from the restrictions that handicapped them in competing with unregulated (or very lightly regulated) financial intermediaries—nonbank banks, in effect.

As regulatory and customary restrictions on risky lending by banks eroded, banks became willing to make "subprime" mortgage loans—a euphemism for mortgage loans to people at high risk of defaulting. (Some of these loans are what are called NINJA loans—no income, no job, no assets, meaning that the borrower does not have to undergo a credit check in advance of the loan's being approved.) Such people tend not to have enough money to make a substantial down payment on a home—so suppose lenders are willing to lend them 100 percent of the purchase price. Many of the borrowers may even have trouble making monthly interest payments—so suppose the loan agreement makes the interest rate vary with the market rate of interest; the borrower pays a low interest rate now but the lender can raise it later if the market rate rises. The required monthly payment may even be set below the interest rate—may even be set at zero for the first two years of the loan—because the borrower cannot afford more. So instead of the mortgage shrinking month by month because the borrower is paying interest and repaying principal, the mortgage grows because the unpaid interest gets added to the principal.

In risky mortgage lending, the lender (more precisely, whoever ends up bearing the risk of a default by the borrower) is more like a partner in a real estate business than like a secured lender. For suppose the value of the home drops, even slightly, before much of the loan has been repaid (and in the early years of the typical mortgage loan, very little of the principal is repaid, because the monthly payments on a mortgage are a fixed amount and the interest component dominates at the outset when none of the principal has yet been repaid). The owner will find himself owing more on the house than it is worth. He may therefore decide to abandon it to the lender. If he had bought the house as a speculation, he may abandon it if its value simply fails to increase. He may *have* to do that, if he was counting on an increase in its value to enable him to refinance the mortgage at a lower interest rate because his equity in the house would be greater.

Risky mortgage lending can be *extremely* risky from the lender's standpoint, because a single default can wipe out the earnings on several good mortgage loans. Suppose that after expenses of foreclosure and brokerage and the like the lender will recover only 60 percent of his loan if the owner defaults. That 40 percent loss could well exceed the annual interest earned on seven or eight mortgage loans of the same size on other houses.

So subprime lenders, and anyone else who had an interest in a subprime mortgage loan, were skating on thin ice. When it broke—because it turned out that they were lending into a housing bubble that would burst long before the mortgages were repaid—many of them were rendered insolvent because of the huge volume of risky mortgage loans. As many as 40 percent of the $3 trillion in mortgage loans made in the United States in 2006 may have been subprime or otherwise of high risk, such as "Alt-A" mortgages, where the borrower has a decent credit rating but there is some other serious risk factor.

As pointed out in a prescient article by the finance theorist Raghuram Rajan in 2005, the attractiveness of risky lending or other risky investing is enhanced by the asymmetrical response of most investors to the good and the bad results of an investment strategy. A strategy that produces good results attracts new investments, and the investment fund grows. If the fund (a trust fund administered by a bank, for example) does poorly, it will lose investors, but generally at a slower rate than it gains them when it does well. Investors tend to stay with a poor performer for a time, either out of inattention or because they are hoping that its performance will improve; whatever attracted them to the fund in the first place may feed that hope.

And because of economies of scale in financial management, the profit margin of an investment fund increases as the fund grows. In a rising market, the fund can grow rapidly—attracting new investors because it is earning high returns while at the same time reducing its average costs—by increasing leverage. "Leverage" is the ratio of debt to equity (borrowed to owned assets) in a firm's capital structure. Because debt is a prescribed sum owed to a creditor regardless of how well or how badly the debtor does, the higher the ratio of debt to equity, the more money a financial firm will make in a rising market—its revenues will rise but not its costs.

As Rajan also pointed out, banks and other financial companies have little incentive, in deciding how much risk to take, to worry about small probabilities of disaster. By definition, low-probability events occur rarely, and if they occur at all it is unlikely to be in the immediate future. Until disaster does occur, the riskiness of the firm's investment strategy, although it may be the cause of the firm's high return, will be invisible to most investors and so it will look as if the firm is generating a high return with low risk. The higher the return on an investment is relative to risk, the more attractive the investment is to a risk-averse investor, and so the better the performance of the financial manager seems.

That is one reason the private sector cannot be expected to adopt measures, such as forbearing to engage in highly risky lending, that might prevent a depression, and thus why preventing depressions has to be a government responsibility. Even though the financial industry has more information bearing on the likelihood of a depression than the government does, it has little incentive to analyze that information. A depression is too remote an event to influence business behavior. Given discounting to present value and the fact that by virtue of the principle of limited liability the creditors of a bankrupt corporation cannot go after the personal assets of the corporation's owners or managers, events that are catastrophic to a corporation if they occur but are highly unlikely to occur, and therefore if they do occur are likely to occur in the distant future, will not influence the corporation's behavior. A bankruptcy is not the end of the world for a company's executives, or even for its shareholders if they have a diversified portfolio of stocks and other assets. But a cascade of bank bankruptcies can be a disaster for a nation.

The more leveraged a bank's (or other financial company's) capital structure is, the greater the risk of insolvency. Whether bank insolvencies, even if they precipitate a stock market crash, will trigger a depression thus depends on how widespread the insolvencies are, how deep the decline in the stock market is, and—of critical, but until the depression was upon us of neglected, importance—how much savings people have.

The balance between consumption and savings is critical to depression analysis. The higher the savings rate, the less likely it is that a difficulty in borrowing, caused by bank insolvencies, and a loss of wealth, caused by a decline in the stock market, will result in a steep reduction in the demand for goods and services. People will dip into their savings to maintain something close to their habitual level of consumption.

To understand the interplay of the depression-inducing factors that I have been discussing, we now need to consider the fundamentals of borrowing and lending, and in particular their relation to consumption and savings. A person who borrows money in order to buy things (a house, a car, etc.) is increasing his present consumption at the expense of his future consumption, because he will have to pay back the loan eventually. The firm that borrows money in order to produce things (build a house, for example) is increasing its present production, though most short-term business borrowing is necessitated simply by the fact that production (cost) normally precedes sale (revenue), and businesses borrow to bridge the gap between expenditure and receipt. Either way, borrowing increases current economic activity. The lower interest rates are, the more borrowing there is and therefore the more buying and selling. When rates are low, you want to be a borrower, not a lender (that is, not a saver). Interest rates were very low in the early 2000s. That was a critical factor in the credit binge that has brought the economy low. A credit binge in the 1920s is widely believed to have been a precipitant of the Great Depression.

A consumer who lends, say by placing some of his money in a money market fund, is reducing his present consumption in order to increase his future consumption; he is saving for the future. Savings are the source of money for lending to other consumers, the ones who want to consume more today. Because borrowing and lending—credit transactions—increase present economic activity, a sudden sharp decline in borrowing and lending reduces that activity—reduces both consumption and production—and can trigger a vicious cycle that produces a high rate of unemployment of both human and capital resources.

That is the principal justification for ex ante regulation of the finance industry. (A subordinate jus-tification is that since the government insures de-mand deposits, it wants to make sure that banks don't take excessive risks with that money.) By "ex ante" regulation I mean regulating behavior before anything bad happens. Speed limits are a form of ex ante regulation; liability for injuring someone in an automobile accident is a form of ex post regula-tion. The latter form of regulation is cheaper be-cause it comes into play only in the relatively rare instances in which a mishap occurs. But it operates on the principle of deterrence—the threat of liabil-ity is assumed to make people more careful—and deterrence is rarely perfect. So when the conse-quences of a single accident can be catastrophic, the emphasis shifts from deterrence to prevention. That is the case concerning mishaps in the finance industry. As we are experiencing, such mishaps can cause economic disaster. Ex ante regulation failed in this instance.

Personal savings might be expected to act as a brake on the vicious cycle that I have been describ-ing, thus reducing the need for regulation. If peo-ple cannot sustain their current level of consump-tion by continued borrowing, because the credit market has seized up, they can reallocate some of their savings to consumption—that is, shift consumption from future to present. But in the years leading up to the current depression, the personal savings rate of Americans had plummeted. From 10 percent in 1980 it dropped into negative territory in 2005 (meaning that people were spending more than they were earning and thus were dissaving) and then fluctuated in a narrow band around zero percent until the financial crisis began inducing people to save more of their income—in December 2008 the personal savings rate rose to 3.6 percent. The drop was natural because, as I said, the lower interest rates are, the more advantageous it is to borrow rather than to save.

The economic significance of the decline in the personal savings rate was masked by the fact that the market value of people's savings, concentrated as those savings were not only in houses but also in common stocks held in brokerage accounts, profit-sharing and retirement accounts, health savings plans, and college savings plans, was rising because house and stock prices were rising, the first vertiginously. But it is important to distinguish between the market value of a person's savings and the composition of the portfolio of assets that constitutes his savings. If the portfolio is risky because it is dominated by risky assets, the market value of the portfolio, and thus of the person's savings, may fall unexpectedly, just like the market value of banks whose asset portfolios had high risk. Even if the market value does not fall a great deal, the expectation created by hard times that it will fall more may cause people to sell their risky assets (thus causing further declines in the market value of those assets) and invest the proceeds in safe assets, or shift some of their income from consumption to savings.

Many people don't have much in the way of savings, risky or safe. They tend to be heavily dependent on credit to finance their consumption, and so when credit dries up they have to cut their personal consumption expenditures drastically.

When a person's wealth increases, he can use the increment to consume more or to invest more, or both; and probably he will use at least some of it to invest more. As the value of a person's house or of his stock portfolio rises, he is likely to buy more stock and more house (maybe a bigger house, or a second home, or improvements to his home). Those are the assets he is familiar with, and as they are doing well, they seem a good investment. The additional investment pushes up the price of stocks and houses, and hence the measured wealth of people who own such assets. Adjusted for risk, however, personal savings will be shrinking along with the savings rate, not growing; more precisely, precautionary (rainy-day) savings will be shrinking. Thus, despite the increase in measured personal wealth in the early 2000s, debt service (interest) as a percentage of personal income rose sharply, though the rise was partly offset by the deductibility of mortgage interest from federal income tax because so much savings was in the form of home-ownership. People's savings were at once smaller relative to their personal consumption expenditures and riskier, and both are reasons that an economic shock would cause a sharp reduction in those expenditures.

When stock prices and especially housing prices plummeted after their steep ascent fueled by cheap credit (as they had to do eventually because they had been driven up not by fundamental economic changes but by expectations that turned out to be mistaken), the market value of personal savings, concentrated in those risky assets, plummeted too. The inadequacy of people's savings was thus exposed; and when savings are inadequate, people who lose their jobs, or cannot sell the houses they can no longer afford, cannot or dare not reallocate savings to consumption. Instead, consumption falls steeply. Some people use money they would otherwise have spent on consumption to rebuild their savings, in order to cope with the uncertainty of their economic future—and indeed, as I have noted, the personal savings rate has soared. Other people, whose incomes have already fallen, reduce their consumption because they do not have enough savings to enable them to maintain their standard of living even if they reallocate all their savings to consumption.

There is a parallel between the behavior of banks and the behavior of consumers, with safe personal savings corresponding to banks' reserves (cash or an account with a federal reserve bank, which is the equivalent of cash) and other safe assets. When savings/safe assets decline to a dangerous level, consumers buy less and banks lend less.

As consumption falls, output falls, precipitating layoffs that further reduce consumption, creating the vicious cycle dramatized by the virtual collapse of the American-owned automobile industry—already in perilous straits because of dwindling demand for gas guzzlers—as people decided to postpone the purchase of new cars. Cheap credit and risky lending had created a kind of automobile bubble—not an increase in the price of automobiles, of course, because the supply of automobiles is much more elastic than that of housing, but rather an increase in the number of automobiles produced, as more people bought second and even third cars and replaced their cars more frequently. U.S. auto sales rose sharply in the early 2000s—a rise inexplicable in terms of fundamental factors—to 17 million in 2005, falling to little more than 13 million in 2008 and expected to be even lower in 2009.

With the economy's output dropping, and therefore corporate profits as well, with no end of the decline in sight and a growing aversion to owning risky assets, it is no surprise that the stock market has plummeted too. Another cause is the need for cash by firms and individuals whose income has declined. The market decline has made people reduce their spending because they are poorer and face greater uncertainty. If they do not need to use their entire reduced income for consumption, the reduction in spending will increase their savings, and what is saved does not contribute to the demand for goods and services.

The timing of the financial crisis, moreover, could not have been worse. It struck during a presidential campaign and deepened during a presidential transition. The lame-duck President seemed uninterested in and uninformed about economic matters and was unable to project an image of leadership and instead spent his final months in office in frequent trips abroad and in legacy-polishing while the domestic economy melted away. Economic officials and private business leaders alike displayed slow uptake and stumbling responses to the financial crisis, undermining confidence in the nation's economic management. And the crisis accelerated during the Christmas shopping season, which normally accounts for 30 to 50 percent of annual retail sales of most goods and services other than food, drugs, and utilities. The buying binge that had been financed by a reduction in safe savings (because savings had been used to buy risky assets like houses and stock) and by heavy borrowing left American consumers awash in consumer durables, and this made it easy for them to postpone buying when the housing bubble and then the credit bubble burst. Consumer durables are more durable than they used to be, moreover, so that replacement—for example of cars—can be deferred without hardship longer than used to be possible.

Furthermore, for many Americans shopping has a recreational aspect, and tastes in recreation can change rapidly. One of the extraordinary aspects of the current economic situation is that buying luxury items has become unfashionable. Many people who can afford to buy such items despite the depression are not doing so.

But wait—since savings are the source of lending, how could a decline in the personal savings rate have coincided with excessive borrowing for personal consumption? Heavy borrowing should increase interest rates, which should in turn reduce the demand for credit. But the Federal Reserve, in reaction to a recession triggered by the collapse, which began in March 2000, of a bubble in dotcom stocks, had used its control over the supply of money to push interest rates way down in order to encourage consumption and production. It kept them down for five years. And the emergence of a global capital surplus kept them low even when the Federal Reserve raised them in 2006. With personal savings by Americans a diminishing source of funds for lending, the slack was taken up by foreign owners of capital, including sovereign (government) loan funds of nations such as China and the major oil-producing countries of the Middle

East that exported much more than they imported and as a result had large dollar surpluses that they were eager to invest.

China's role in setting the stage for the current crisis has received a good deal of criticism. The criticism is that by depreciating its currency relative to the dollar, China made its products very cheap to businesses and consumers in the United States and U.S. products very expensive to Chinese businesses and consumers. The story is more complicated. Chinese incomes are very low; few Chinese can afford our goods. And China is not the only major country that exports much more to the United States than it imports from us and reinvests its surplus dollars in this country. Japan and Germany are others—German state banks were big buyers of mortgage-backed securities originated by American banks.

When domestic demand is weak, moreover, as in China, encouraging exports is a way of achieving fuller employment of productive resources. We are in that position today. Our domestic demand is weak. Would that we could offset that weakness with brisk exporting. We cannot because—in another frightening resemblance to the Great Depression—we are in a *global* depression, which has reduced the demand for our exports.

Throughout the early 2000s, we were flooded with foreign capital. Our chronic trade deficit swelled. We were living on credit. That is a precarious state for a nation, as it is for an individual. But it is a delicious state for lenders, and therefore banks. One might think that low interest rates would hurt as well as help lenders, since competition would limit how much banks could charge for loans. But the banking industry can make more money by borrowing at 2 percent and lending at 6 percent than by borrowing at 6 percent and lending at 10 percent, because the lower the interest rate paid by borrowers, the greater the demand for loans.

It would be a mistake, however, to think that because the world was awash in money, the Federal Reserve had lost control over interest rates — that countries that had large dollar balances that they chose to invest in the United States were to blame for our low interest rates. Had the Federal Reserve feared inflation in 2000, it would have used its control over U.S. banks to raise interest rates. It was able to raise those rates in 2006 notwithstanding the continued influx of foreign capital.

2

The Crisis in Banking

WHEN SECRETARY OF THE TREASURY Henry Paulson in September 2008 first proposed a $700 billion bailout of financial institutions, he assumed that the problem besetting the banks was illiquidity—an inability to transform assets into cash—rather than insolvency. That was a mistake, and a mistake that went to the heart of the financial crisis. But to see this will require amplification of the earlier discussion of the nature of banking. Banking is an unusual business; a proper understanding of it is central to an understanding of our economic troubles.

Financial intermediaries—"banks" in my extended sense—are big borrowers as well as big lenders, for what they mainly lend is money they have borrowed. (Demand deposits, for example, are loans to banks that the lenders—the depositors—can demand immediate repayment of.) Funded as they are out of borrowed money, banks' loans greatly exceed their equity capital—the assets they own rather than borrow. That capital is their cushion against bankruptcy. They need a cushion because bank debt is a fixed liability—the money a bank owes its depositors and other lenders (deposits no longer being the major source of banks' capital) does not vary with how well or how badly the bank does—but the revenue that the bank obtains from lending out its borrowed money is variable. It varies not only with interest rates but also with default rates. The risk of default is a major reason that a bank can charge a higher interest rate on its loans than it pays its depositors or other lenders. Defaults if widespread may greatly reduce a bank's revenues, and yet its obligation to repay its lenders will remain what it was. It has to charge a high interest rate to compensate it for the risk of default by the persons or firms to which it lends.

The equity cushion thus reduces the risk of bankruptcy. Suppose a bank owns riskless assets, such as short-term U.S. Treasury bills, of $200 million, and borrows $800 million and lends out the entire amount it has borrowed. It will be able to repay its depositors and other lenders so long as the loans it makes retain three quarters of their value.

Three quarters of $800 million in loans is $600 million, which when added to the equity cushion of $200 million equals what the bank owes its lenders—$800 million. Only if its loan portfolio loses more than 25 percent of its value will the bank be in trouble (in fact insolvent, because its liabilities will exceed its assets).

Being financed to a large extent by short-term credit, banks would be highly vulnerable to "runs" if they took no safety precautions. If a bank seemed to be in trouble, depositors would rush to withdraw their deposits before the bank went broke, and if enough depositors withdrew their money the bank *would* go broke even if, before the run, its assets exceeded its liabilities. Banks were (and are) required to keep a specified percentage of their deposits (usually 10 percent, although the percentage varies from time to time and bank to bank) in riskless assets—cash and cash equivalents. These are a bank's "reserves." They reduce the likelihood of bankruptcy by reducing the volatility of bank capital, but do not eliminate the possibility of a run based on a real or imagined fear of bankruptcy. Federal insurance of demand deposits was created in order to do that. Concern lest banks take advantage of the insurance to make ever-riskier loans—

since the insurance shifted the risk of default from the depositors to the Federal Deposit Insurance Corporation—amplified the need to make banking safe. Consistent with that need, banks used most of their capital other than their reserves either to buy government securities or to make short-term business and personal loans. Long-term bank lending was limited because the bank's liabilities to its depositors were short-term. The depositors could withdraw their money at any time, but the banks could not call any long-term loans (before the loans matured) that they made unless and until there was a default. The bank regulatory agencies limited competition among banks and with non-bank lenders in a further effort to reduce the risk of bank insolvency.

Residential mortgages, which are long-term, were made mainly by savings and loan associations (or mutual savings banks, which were similar), a specialized type of bank operating under strict regulation as well. Despite regulation, S&Ls engaged in risky mortgage lending (partly because federal deposit insurance was not "experience rated"—the insurance premium was invariant to the riskiness of the bank's lending) and went broke en masse in the 1980s for a variety of reasons that included a real estate bust. This was a further illustration of the instability of credit markets, especially credit markets linked to real estate, and thus an unheeded warning sign of the disaster to come.

Despite the bad experience with the S&Ls, "safety first" regulation of commercial banks continued to be whittled down as part of the deregulation movement that had begun in the 1970s. Brokerage firms and investment banks, such as Merrill Lynch and Lehman Brothers, which were not regulated as banks, along with other nonbank financial intermediaries such as finance companies, money market funds, and hedge funds, were increasingly permitted to offer financial products similar or even identical to those of banks. Their borrowed capital, unlike bank deposits, was not federally insured, and hence these nonbank lenders were highly vulnerable to runs. Because they offered a number of financial products besides bank-like products, competition impelled and regulators permitted banks to offer the same products so that they wouldn't lose too much business to the growing nonbank industry, which by 2008 was almost as large as the commercial-banking industry. But federal insurance of demand deposits remained, which by reducing the threat of "a run on the bank" further encouraged risk taking. One reason that hedge funds have not encountered problems of solvency as acute as those of commercial banks may be that no part of their capital is federally insured, so they have to worry that if they have too much leverage in their capital structure, or otherwise overdo risk, they will face a run (as some have).

A largely unregulated banking industry—for "banking" had become virtually synonymous with financial intermediation—converged, fatally as it has turned out, with falling interest rates in the early 2000s. By 2003 the average interest rate for a six-month certificate of deposit had fallen to 1.17 percent, the average thirty-year mortgage rate to 5.83 percent, and the average rate for an adjustable-rate mortgage (a mortgage loan in which the interest rate is periodically reset) to 3.76 percent. The low rates caused the demand for credit to soar. Borrowing, as we know, increases economic activity. One form the increased activity took was increased home building and buying. House prices rose. Real estate investing is traditionally debt-heavy because real estate is an excellent form of collateral, so the demand for mortgage loans rose with house prices.

Leverage, which we met in chapter 1, is doubly

attractive when interest rates are low and investment values are rising. Suppose a firm that has equity of $1 million and no debt makes loans that yield an annual return of 7 percent. So the firm earns $70,000 a year. Now let it borrow $2 million at 3 percent interest ($60,000 a year) and invest its total assets of $3 million in similar loans. Seven percent of $3 million is $210,000, and after subtracting the interest expense of $60,000 the firm has annual earnings of $150,000—more than double its earnings before it borrowed. With low interest rates and rising real estate (and other asset) values, the banking industry increased its leverage. Low interest rates increase the demand for borrowing and at the same time make it cheaper for lenders to meet the increased demand by increasing their borrowing than by raising equity capital. So their leverage rises.

Attractive as it is, leverage is also dangerous. If the firm in my example has a bad year, in which the return on the loans it makes is a negative 5 percent, the firm will lose $50,000 (5 percent of $1 million) if it has not borrowed anything, but it will lose $210,000 if it has borrowed $2 million: $150,000, the loss on the $3 million in loans that it has made, plus $60,000, the interest on its $2 million loan.

(Both the upside and the downside of leverage arise from the simple fact that the obligation created by a debt is fixed. It does not rise when revenue rises, but neither does it fall when revenue declines.) A highly leveraged lender (a nonbank lender might have a debt-to-equity ratio of 30 to 1, or even higher, but even a commercial bank's debt-to-equity ratio might reach 25 to 1), lending to a highly leveraged borrower, such as a first-time home buyer with heavy debt, a low income, and no savings, is courting financial disaster. It has a risky capital structure that it is making riskier by committing its capital to extremely risky loans.

What made leverage even more dangerous for banks during the housing bubble was that rather than retaining the mortgages they had originated or bought, they sold most of them in exchange for securities backed by those mortgages. Sometimes they packaged the mortgages themselves and issued their own securities backed by them; and slices of these securities, as of similar securities issued by other firms, often were bought by other banks. Mortgage-backed securities thus became a part of banks' equity capital. If because of defaults by mortgagors the value of the securities (which depended on the interest paid by the mortgagors) fell, the banks' equity would be impaired.

The mortgage-backed securities were believed to be quite safe. Some were. Many banks that originated mortgages sold them to Fannie Mae or Freddie Mac in exchange for securities backed by prime mortgages guaranteed by Fannie and Freddie. But there was a problem with securities backed in part by subprime mortgages (including Alt-A and other highly risky mortgages). Such securities were bought and sold by other financial intermediaries, but commercial banks got into the act by packaging and selling securities backed by subprime mortgages. When the housing bubble burst and the subprime mortgage market collapsed, banks found themselves with an unsalable inventory of securities that they had created but could sell, if at all, only at fire-sale prices.

To understand why mortgage-backed securities were considered safe even when backed by subprime as well as prime mortgages, we must note to begin with that such securities are not what come to mind when one hears the word "security." Each security was priced at hundreds of millions of dollars and sometimes at more than a billion dollars and was backed by hundreds or even thousands of residential mortgages—"backed" in the sense that the security entitled its owners to the revenue from the mortgages; the value of the security thus depended on the mortgage revenue. The pooling of the mortgages that backed each security diversified the risk of default geographically and thus reduced it; a rise in defaults in Florida might be offset by a decline in defaults in New York.

So far, so good, as far as management of risk was concerned. In addition, each security was sliced into different risk-return combinations and a purchaser could pick the one he wanted. (In other words, *shares* in each security were sold.) The top tier would have the first claim on the income generated by the pool of mortgages that backed the security, and so it had the highest credit rating and paid the lowest interest rate. The bottom tier would have the last claim on the income of the pool, and so it had the lowest credit rating and paid the highest interest rate. (The tiers are called "tranches," but I avoid the term as I do other financial jargon.)

The simplest way to visualize the tiered structure is to pretend that a mortgage-backed security is a house with a first and second mortgage on it. The first mortgagee is protected as long as the second mortgage is not completely wiped out, and the second mortgagee is protected as long as the owner of the mortgaged property does not default. (There were more than three tiers of risk in mortgage-backed securities; I use three merely as an illustration.) A first mortgage corresponds to the top tier of a mortgage-backed security, a second mortgage to the middle tier, and the owner's equity to the bottom tier. Suppose the first mortgage is $1 million, the second mortgage $500,000, and the owner's equity $500,000, so that the total value of the house is $2 million. And suppose the owner defaults and the house will fetch only $1,250,000 in a foreclosure sale. The second mortgagee will foreclose and the house will be sold at the foreclosure sale for $1,250,000. The owner will lose his entire equity, the second mortgagee will lose half his investment, but the first mortgagee will lose nothing, since the price at the foreclosure sale exceeded the value of his investment.

So mortgage-backed securities are nothing like shares of stock; functionally they are bonds secured by (and in fact constituting) fractional shares of mortgages of varying degrees of risk.

The mortgages in each pool that backed up a mortgage-backed security would be selected in such a way that the top tier would get a triple-A credit rating from a credit-rating agency, based on the perceived unlikelihood that so many of the mortgages in the pool would go into default that the lower tiers could not absorb the entire loss. (Sometimes more than one tier had a triple-A rating, but I'll ignore that detail.) This meant that the top tier of a mortgage-backed security could earn a triple-A credit rating even if it was backed by few, or indeed no, prime mortgages. For the smaller the top tier, the more defaults there could be before there was not enough value in the entire pool of mortgages backing the security to satisfy the claims of the top tier's owners.

Conventional banks tended to buy the top tier in each mortgage-backed security, while nonbank financial intermediaries, being willing to bear greater risk, tended to buy lower tiers. Many of the purchasers made assurance doubly sure—they thought—by purchasing credit-default swaps, a form of insurance that I'll discuss shortly.

The housing bubble that began in the late 1990s, though it was not of uniform magnitude geographically, was so widespread that geographical diversification did not reduce the overall risk of mortgage defaults sufficiently to avert a calamitous fall in the value of the mortgage-backed securities when the housing bubble burst. The fall in housing prices and the rise in defaults and foreclosures (which had been, as one would expect, at a low level when prices were rising) were so steep that even triple-A tiers of mortgage-backed securities soon traded at less than half their estimated value.

The geographical diversification produced by securitization had *some* effect in mitigating the financial crisis that securitization, by loading up the banks' balance sheets with assets that turned out to be exceedingly risky, had helped produce. The fall in housing values and the resulting surge of defaults and foreclosures have been concentrated in states like California, Arizona, Nevada, and Florida. The State of California is on the brink of insolvency and might well be over it by now had securitization not spread some of the costs of defaults by California mortgagors to other states.

This raises the question of how big a role securitization actually played in bringing about the economic crisis. Risky lending (for example, requiring purchasers of stock on credit to put up collateral equal to only 10 percent of the loan) brought on the Great Depression without benefit of securitized debt. Had banks retained on their books subprime and Alt-A mortgages rather than securitizing them or buying mortgage-backed securities from other securitizers, would they be better off today? If so, this would be due primarily to the power of securitization to attract additional capital to the U.S. housing industry from investors (especially foreign investors) who would not want the bother of actually owning someone's mortgage, and the complexity of the mortgage-backed securities, which made their riskiness hard to assess. But if low interest rates and a strong demand for credit encouraged risky lending (as they did), the form in which mortgage loans was held may not have been a critical factor in the collapse of the banks.

The opacity of complex securities to investors to one side, there is nothing improper about securitizing debt—that is, transforming a debt into a security. Suppose a bank has made a loan secured by a thirty-year mortgage. Rather than wait thirty years to recover principal and interest, the bank might want to sell the mortgage for its discounted present value (reflecting the fact that a dollar today is worth more than the expectation of receiving a dollar in the future) so that it would have more money to lend. An issuer of a security that pools many purchased mortgages and gives the buyers fractional shares in the pool may obtain a higher return than if he sold the mortgage to another bank. Not only may pooling reduce through diversification the risk of default and thus make the investment safer, but the less-protected tiers of the securities can be marketed to investors who like risk more than banks, or some banks, do.

A neglected downside of distributing risk, however, is that it spreads risk to what would otherwise be safe markets. Mortgage-backed securities, traded all over the world, brought the riskiness of residential-mortgage loans made during the U.S. housing bubble to foreign banks and other foreign investors and thus helped to globalize what might have been just a U.S. depression. There would have been some negative effects on the economies of foreign countries, given the size of our economy. But securitization made it possible to obtain credit from foreign lenders who would not have wanted to own mortgages on homes in the United States (or other private debt), with all the attendant contractual and administrative complexities, but were happy to buy securities backed by mortgages and rated triple A by accredited credit-rating agencies. The securities were also bought by U.S. insurance companies, pension funds, and other investors that would not have been comfortable dealing directly with mortgagors either.

Other forms of debt were securitized—mortgages on commercial real estate, but also debt unrelated to real estate, such as credit card debt and student loans. For simplicity I confine my analysis to securities backed by residential mortgages, in part because the other debt securitizations seem, with a lag, to be following securities backed by residential mortgages into the toilet. Those securities first lost value because of the bursting of the housing bubble, precipitating an economic downturn that has engulfed other debt, securitized and nonsecuritized, as well.

That credit agencies were willing to rate mortgage-backed securities enabled purchasers (they thought!) to take as much or as little risk as was prudent in their particular circumstances. But they also could, and many did, buy a form of insurance, issued in great quantity by, among many other firms, the American International Group, against declines in the value of mortgage-backed securities, as well as of other investments. This form of insurance, called "credit-default swaps," had originally been intended as insurance against bond defaults, of which there was a long history on the basis of which premiums could be computed with reasonable confidence. But AIG and other financial firms (not limited to insurance companies and commercial banks, the traditional issuers of credit insurance, such as conventional mortgage insurance, as distinct from insurance of securitized debt) began issuing credit-default swaps to insure against losses in the value of mortgage-backed securities, which lacked such a history. One beauty of swaps was that they reduced the amount of collateral that a lender needed in order to protect itself from the consequence of the borrower's default. Instead of insisting on collateral as protection against the consequences of default, the lender could pay the premium on a credit-default swap.

Swaps were thought to (and often did) reduce a lender's risk, allowing greater leverage and therefore higher returns with no apparent increase in risk. And the swaps themselves became securitized, so that institutions all over the world became insurers of mortgage-backed securities. In their securitized form, moreover, the swaps could be bought by entities that had no assets that they wanted to insure but merely wanted to speculate on the possibility of a default by the firm insured by a swap. Soon the face value of the swaps was in the tens of trillions of dollars. The swaps were not regulated, and so the issuers, unlike insurance companies, which were regulated, were not required to have reserves against having to make good on defaults that the swaps insured against. AIG's reserves turned out to be insufficient to cover its liabilities when defaults insured by its swaps soared.

Banks were among the purchasers of securitized credit swaps, which made them insurers—often of other banks. This was dangerous: having to honor the swap might break a bank, and if the bank defaulted this would deprive the bank on the other side of the credit swap of insurance needed to protect its solvency. There would be a domino effect.

The credit-rating agencies and the issuers of credit-default swaps had great difficulty determining the value of mortgage-backed securities. Investors had limited information about the riskiness of individual mortgages, and there was insufficient experience with large-scale subprime lending to enable the risk of default of subprime mortgages to be assessed with any confidence; risk assessment had to be based on models rather than on experience. Credit-rating agencies, like insurance companies, perforce estimate risk mainly by looking at past experience, and such limited experience as there was with mortgage-backed securities had been acquired during a period of rising house prices. Banks that packaged and sold mortgage-backed securities had little incentive to make careful estimates of the riskiness of the mortgages that backed the securities, because sale shifted the risk of default to the purchasers of the securities. Prospective purchasers had an incentive to assess that risk, of course, but they had less information than the originators.

A bank that owned a share in a mortgage-backed security could not readily determine the value of all the different mortgages that backed it because the bank would have no relationship with the borrowers even if it had originated some of the mortgages. The originator or purchaser would have hired mortgage-servicing companies to collect payments of principal and interest from the mortgagors and to foreclose if the mortgagors defaulted. With each security having multiple owners, the foreclosure rate of mortgages that backed mortgage-backed securities was apt to be unusually high. The servicer had conflicting duties to his many masters, which complicated his efforts to modify a mortgage in default and thus avoid having to foreclose (especially when mortgages on many houses are foreclosed at the same time, foreclosures sales are likely to yield meager returns for the mortgagee). The owner of the triple-A tier of the security might be happy with a modification of the merger that would obviate the need for foreclosure and avoid a loss to him, even if it wiped out the lower tiers. But the owners of those tiers might press for foreclosure in the hope that a foreclosure sale would produce enough to give them something. Such conflicts complicated servicers' efforts to renegotiate mortgages that were in default.

To understand how the difficulty of determining the riskiness of the new financial instruments contributed to the financial crisis, it is helpful to recall a distinction, made long ago by the economist Frank Knight, between two types of risk. One, which he called "risk," is a risk to which a probability can be assigned, and is the kind that insurance companies insure against because they can calculate a premium that will cover the risk. The other, called "uncertainty," is a risk that cannot be quantified. Anyone who insures such a risk is gambling; anyone who rates it (AAA, BB, etc.) is guessing.

Because the banking industry was highly leveraged, and because much of its capital consisted of securities that were very difficult to value, the bursting of the housing bubble shrank the banks' capital—but by an unknown amount because of the valuation problem. The banks didn't know how meager their equity cushion had become and therefore how much they could lend without incurring a high risk of bankruptcy, since as we know lending is increasingly risky the more leverage the lender has in its capital structure. A further complication was that banks that had bought the insurance side of credit-default swaps did not know their exposure. When Lehman Brothers collapsed, issuers of credit-default swaps all over the world were on the hook because Lehman had purchased many swaps. It had issued many swaps as well, and its equity, devoured by the collapse of the mortgage-backed securities, which it had held in great quantity, was insufficient to enable it to pay the debts that it had insured.

Suppose bank A had insured Lehman against a loss of $X, and bank B was insured by Lehman against a loss of $X. Then A should have given B $X, rather than both getting entangled in Lehman's bankruptcy. But the bankruptcy was so sudden that the A's and the B's didn't have time to find each other, and so were left uncertain about their position in light of the bankruptcy.

One reason a company can find itself in a death

spiral is the common provision in loan agreements that requires the borrower to put up more collateral if his credit rating falls. When American International Group's liability on credit-default swaps began to balloon, the credit-rating agencies reduced the company's credit rating. By requiring AIG to post more collateral, the rating change deepened the company's woes to the point where death was averted only by an infusion of almost $130 billion in federal bailout money—a number that may grow.

The banks' uncertainty about the value of their mortgage-related assets and swap insurance and the magnitude of their swap liabilities curtailed— indeed, until the government stepped in, froze— lending. That was the "credit crunch." It caused both an immediate drop in economic activity and, in reaction to that drop and in anticipation of a further drop in the near future, a precipitous decline in the stock market. It started the dangerous spiral that we're in.

Ordinarily one would expect a credit crunch to be self-correcting. A shortage of capital for lending, due to the shrinkage of the banks' equity cushion, would attract new capital to banking, to rebuild the cushion. But that would depend on how much the cushion had shrunk and whether the crunch had so damaged the economy that the demand for loans would drop. In fact the banks were unable to attract enough new private capital to assure their solvency. Warren Buffett's $5 billion loan to Goldman Sachs in September 2008 was an exception—Mitsubishi's $9 billion investment in Morgan Stanley the following month was not, because it was guaranteed by the federal government.

At least until the U.S. dollar ceases to be the world's principal reserve currency (a currency held by foreign banks as well as by the issuing country's own banks, and used as a major medium for international transactions), the federal government has almost unlimited capital because of its taxing, borrowing, and money-creating powers, and it is not constrained by having to make a profit or even cover its costs to survive. Government officials thought at first that the credit crunch was the result of a kind of panic—that the banks were scared to lend because they didn't know how thick their equity cushion was. If so, then by buying the mortgage-backed securities from the banks the government would dispel the panic and unfreeze lending. It would need to hold the securities that it had bought only until their value became clear; it would then sell them and recover the purchase price. This was the thinking behind the first bailout bill (the Emergency Economic Stabilization Act of 2008), passed early in October 2008.

Imagine that you have a very valuable sculpture but no one will consider buying it because it is erroneously suspected of having been stolen. Although the sculpture was valuable before the suspicion arose and will again be valuable as soon as the suspicion is dispelled, at the moment there is no market for it. It is unsalable not because it isn't valuable but because it is illiquid—impossible to exchange for cash—and it is illiquid because the market is not working. Liquidity can be restored, even while the right to sell the sculpture is in doubt, if some collector is willing to buy the sculpture for a price discounted to reflect the cloud on the seller's right to sell it.

Banks' mortgage-backed securities were thought to be illiquid and therefore unsalable because of uncertainty about the values of those securities. The risk of default of the mortgages that backed those securities, and hence the current value of the securities, could not be estimated, for want of comparable historical experience. Not enough investors were willing to gamble on these securities of uncertain value to create a market for them; a prospective buyer who has little information about a product that someone wants to sell him, and who cannot rely on a warranty or on the seller's concern with reputation to assure that the product represents a good value, will be reluctant to buy. An investor might even hesitate to buy a mortgage-backed security not because he doubted the valuation placed on it by the seller but because he would look bad if it turned out to be a poor investment—he would be said not to have learned his lesson. It is the same kind of thinking that has led the government to invest excessively in airline security since the 9/11 attacks; the failure to prevent an exact repetition of those attacks could not, however rational, escape extreme censure.

For want of a market for its mortgage-backed securities, a bank could not exchange them for assets of known value and so could not determine how much equity it had and therefore how much it could safely lend. The safest course was to lend nothing and instead place its capital in federal government securities, especially since, even if the value of the risky assets could be estimated, the estimate could so easily be mistaken that the bank would lack confidence in it; the estimated value would just be the midpoint of a wide distribution of possible values.

The bank would have to reckon with a substantial probability that the actual value of its assets would turn out to be far below the best estimate of their value.

Not having to worry about going broke by making an improvident purchase, the reasoning went, the government could buy the banks' opaque assets and thereby dispel the banks' paralyzing anxiety. But this would not work if the problem was not that a bank's assets were frozen or, even if liquid, too risky to be considered a secure part of the bank's equity cushion and therefore a secure basis for lending, but that they were worth very little. For then if the government bought them at the best (though by assumption a virtually arbitrary) estimate of their value, its action would simply expose the banks' insolvency in its nakedness for all the world to peer at appalled, while if it bought them for more than a defensible estimate of their value it would be enriching the banks' shareholders at the expense of the innocent taxpayer. And it would be enriching the shareholders of the worst banks—the banks with the sickest assets—the most, and thus setting a very bad example for future failing firms that might come running to Uncle Sam for help.

The fact that the triple-A-rated tiers of mortgage-backed securities were marked down to about 40 percent of their face value, when the mortgage default rate was only 15 percent, has been offered as further evidence that maybe the market had over-reacted to the financial crisis—had "panicked." Yet the markdown may just have reflected an expectation that the default rate would rise. Housing prices had risen so high during the bubble period and fallen so low since that even someone who had bought a house during the bubble and put down a substantial down payment might find that the unpaid balance of his mortgage exceeded the value of his house. He might have put down a 20 percent down payment when he bought the house for $500,000 two years earlier yet the house might now be worth only 70 percent of what he had paid for it. If so, he would have a $400,000 mortgage (minus the small amount of principal that he would have repaid in the first two years of the mortgage) on a house worth only $350,000.

It soon became evident that the banks' problem was not so much illiquidity resulting from uncertainty as it was insolvency, both actual and potential. Some banks were broke and others—perhaps most others, at least weighted by size, since it was the big banks that had found the risky assets most attractive to invest in because they were best able to hedge risk—were on the verge of going broke. Accounting rules required the banks to mark down the value of their mortgage-backed securities and other exotic assets to a reasonable estimate of their current market value. This revaluation process ("mark to market") exposed the banks' parlous financial state with alarming clarity. Fear of insolvency rather than fear of the unknown was the basic reason that banks were unwilling to lend. Even banks with solid balance sheets needed more and sounder capital, because the business environment had become riskier. So the original bailout plan was abruptly altered (the United States embarrassedly taking its cues from the prime minister of the United Kingdom) from a purchase of assets to a contribution of capital to banks, in exchange for which the government received preferred stock in the banks. (Recently the original plan has been revived in an altered form, as we shall see in chapter 5.)

The market test for whether a company's distress is due to illiquidity or insolvency is how the prices of its "frozen" assets move over time. If the low market prices of mortgage-backed securities were not true market values, because the market wasn't working, those prices should have risen by now. They have not done so. This indicates that the basic problem was insolvency.

Even if a combination of uncertainty, the conversion of the major investment banks to bank holding companies, and the high rate of hedge fund redemptions had merely paralyzed the capital markets temporarily, the government would have been criticized for buying the banks' questionable securities for much more than their current, depressed market value, though the purchase might turn out to be a good investment. And if the government paid just the depressed current market value of the assets (so far as it could be estimated, however roughly), then whatever had brought that value so low, the purchase of the assets by the government at their distressed price would merely have confirmed the banks' perilous state.

When the purchase of mortgage-backed and other opaque securities was changed to an infusion of capital, Secretary of the Treasury Paulson, who executed that awkward pivot, further muddied the waters by pleading with the banks that received the infusion to lend it rather than hoard it. That was a futile exercise in jawboning. Banks are in the business of lending. Normally they obtain no return on money that they hoard (by, for example, buying short-term Treasury notes that carry a very low interest rate—today virtually zero). They don't need prodding to make loans—unless the risks are too great, in which event the prodding will be and should be ineffectual. Or unless there is deflation, for then cash grows in value—in purchasing power—without being lent or otherwise invested. That is an alternative, and especially worrisome, explanation for the banks' hoarding cash, though probably not the main explanation. It is worrisome not only because deflation is so dangerous but also because it is a temptation not limited to undercapitalized banks.

Bank lending never shut down completely. Most banks, I believe, honored the standby lines of credit that they had issued, lent to their best customers, and lent to at least a few new customers with sterling credit ratings. What they mainly did was stiffen their credit criteria, which automatically reduced the amount of lending they did, and raise their interest rates, which had the same effect.

Before the banks could prudently resume their old, laxer lending, they had to plump up their equity cushion, and that seems to be mainly what they have used the government's capital infusions for (not that a purchase of preferred stock, the principal form in which the government has invested in the banks, is technically equity, but it is a safe addition to capital because there is no maturity date). That is why it would be a mistake to force them to lend—it could knock them into the abyss of insolvency. Indeed, for safety's sake the banks had to use the bailout money to enlarge their equity cushion (rather than to make loans) *beyond* what it had been before the crash, because loans were now riskier. This was not only because of rising unemployment, which made loans to individuals riskier, but also because of falling output. When a company's output declines, its revenues are less likely to cover its debts and any other fixed costs and so it will be less likely to be able to repay any new loan that it obtains. Falling output, due in part to difficulty in borrowing to buy a car, made it impossible for the Detroit automakers to repay their existing loans, let alone borrow new money. With their bonds trading at a fraction of face value, implying a high probability of default, what rational lender would lend them more money?

Bond prices fell throughout the economy in anticipation of defaults. But the higher return that buyers of the bonds obtained (the less you pay for a bond with a fixed interest rate, the higher the return on your investment) did not attract the banks but merely reminded them how risky lending had become.

A Wall Street financier who prefers to remain nameless has vividly described the quandary in which the banks have found themselves:

> Consider a conservative bank with limited subprime loans and money from the TARP [Troubled Assets Relief Program—the $700 billion bailout program] and access to the Fed's discount window. Such a bank—to the extent it exists—should be doing a healthy business of new loans, taking advantage of the spread between cheap money from the government and current rates on new loans to the private corporate market. But as the bank president looks at the steady stream of bad economic news, he remembers that a sharp decline in GDP will lead to a sharp rise in unemployment, which he knows is well correlated to defaults on even prime mortgages. Suddenly, his book of mortgages, which had always seemed conservative, seems slightly at risk. Then he turns to his corporate loan book, com-

posed of loans to small local businesses and bigger regional operations. Standards for lending had remained high at his bank, even as they'd dipped their toes into construction loans here and there. But then he gazes at the maturities of these loans and notices that some of the loans are coming due in the near term. He also sees that some of these companies have secondary loans, or even unsecured bonds, that are coming due. If capital markets remain frozen, then where will the companies get the capital to refinance these loans? This particular bank president knows that he is ill-equipped to take these companies through bankruptcy (and trade his debt for equity), meaning that he'll have no choice but to renew the loans when they come due in order to keep the companies from filing. Taken together, it makes little sense for him to originate any new loans at this time, considering that he still has very little window into the values of his assets or the future needs of existing lenders. Knowing what might happen to his bank if it ever showed the slightest sign of impaired reserves, our hypothetical bank president decides to hoard his TARP money, and forgo borrowing from the Fed, until visibility is better. This is the conversation going on in banks across America—from Citi to small regionals—and it means that the government's attempt at a liquidity shower is going to do little to actually stimulate lending.

3

The Underlying Causes

I HAVE SUGGESTED that the immediate causes of the depression were the confluence of risky lending with inadequate personal savings, so that when the risks materialized, causing bank insolvencies and a fall in demand for goods and services because credit was difficult to obtain, people couldn't reallocate savings to consumption, and this allowed the fall in demand to trigger a downward spiral in employment and output. Digging a little deeper, we find the housing bubble, the bursting of which produced the defaults that endangered the solvency of the banks; the very low interest rates that motivated the banks to increase their leverage; the complicated financial instruments that turned out to be riskier than people thought; and the withering of regulation of financial services, which removed checks on risky lending. (The bursting of the housing bubble also of course caused the residential-construction market to nose-dive, but it is the broader decline in demand for goods and services that poses the big threat to the economy.) These phenomena too need to be explained rather than just assumed, if there is to be hope of heading off future depressions, and of a prompt recovery from this one.

Among the deep causes of a depression might be human errors—maybe errors of a kind to which people are predisposed by quirks of human cognitive psychology—or character flaws, such as "greed" (whatever that means). It is widely believed, for example, that banks miscalculated the safety of the novel financial instruments, or were taken in by the credit-rating agencies' giving triple-A ratings to what really were risky assets; and that the housing bubble was due to the inability of ordinary people to understand the risks involved in novel forms of mortgage loan, such as a mortgage loan that does not require the borrower to have any equity in his home and does not give him the security of a fixed interest rate. It has been suggested that bubbles reflect irrational optimism or perhaps an inability even of financial professionals to base predictions on anything more sophisticated than simple extrapolation, so that if house values or stock values are rising, the financial markets as well as the consuming public expect them to keep rising indefinitely. One even hears it said that financiers are stupid.

I am skeptical that readily avoidable mistakes, failures of rationality, or the intellectual deficiencies of financial managers whose IQs exceed my own were major factors in the economic collapse. Had the mistakes that brought down the banking industry been *readily* avoidable, they would have been avoided. There were plenty of warnings of a housing bubble, beginning in 2003; warnings about excessive leverage in financial firms; and even rather precise predictions of the debacle that has ensued, as in "When Bubbles Burst," an eerily prescient paper by Thomas Helbling and Marco Terrones published in October 2003. Robert Shiller wrote a similar paper in April of the following year, as did another economist, Avinash Persaud, the same month. The *Economist* magazine spotted the housing bubble in September 2002 and soon became obsessed with it and its possible broader implications for the financial system and the U.S. economy as a whole; in an article published on July 3, 2004, we read: "Housing optimists dismiss these fears by pointing out that doomsters such as *The*

Economist began wringing their hands about a property bubble a year ago, and yet prices have continued to climb. But this has made the housing market not safer, but more vulnerable. The first law of bubbles is that they inflate for a lot longer than anybody expects. The second law is that they eventually burst." A particularly good piece, called "Will It Be Different This Time?," ran in the *Economist* in October of 2004. The *Financial Times* soon picked up the thread. The fragility of the banking system and the inadequacy of banking regulation were related topics discussed frequently in the financial press.

The banks must have known as much as economists and financial journalists did about their industry. They had to know that there was a lot of risk in their capital structures, that the future doesn't always repeat the past and therefore that models of default risk based on historical experience in the housing and credit markets might be unreliable, that credit-rating agencies have a conflict of interest because they're paid by the firms they rate, and that financial intermediation is inherently unstable because to be profitable it usually requires borrowing short-term and lending long-term. So what were the bankers to do? In gauging the risk of calamity, the key probabilities they had to consider were that the rise in housing prices was a bubble and that if it burst house prices would fall by at least 20 percent. If both events came to pass, insolvency would loom. Suppose the best guess was that there was a 10 percent probability that the price rise was a bubble and the same probability that if it was a bubble house prices would fall by at least 20 percent. Then the probability that house prices would fall by at least 20 percent was only 1 percent (0.1 × 0.1), and so disaster would be unlikely to occur for many years, and so the risk of disaster would have seemed worth running. A 1 percent risk of bankruptcy is not like a 1 percent risk of a nuclear war. Bankruptcy is common enough, in fact is an indispensable institution of a capitalist society. Because risk and return are positively correlated, a firm that plays it too safe is, paradoxically, courting failure because investors will turn elsewhere. Businesses must assume a positive though small risk of bankruptcy. A cascade of bank bankruptcies can bring the economy to a halt, but no individual bank has an incentive to take measures to avoid such a consequence.

We need to consider intrafirm conflicts of interest if we want to obtain a better understanding of how the rational decisions of intelligent people can lead to disaster. Banks employ risk managers as well as traders (I include in the term "traders" loan officers and anyone else who makes lending or investment decisions for the bank). But the two types of employee have inherently conflicting objectives—profit for the traders, safety for the risk managers—and these are reciprocals: more profit, less safety. Risk management, unlike trading, is generally not treated as a profit center in a firm, because it is difficult to attribute profits to risk managers, just as it is difficult to attribute profits to the firm's accountants and lawyers, who also are risk managers in effect. Hence a financial firm will tend to give more weight to the views of successful traders than to those of risk managers.

With the rapid expansion of the financial sector in the early 2000s, young, inexperienced traders and analysts achieved positions of responsibility in banks before they were fully prepared by training and experience. And when an organization expands rapidly there is bound to be some loss of control over subordinates, which exacerbates the problem of having a less experienced staff. This is not to blame the financial crisis on the young. Often, perhaps typically, the decision to ramp up the

level of risk in a bank's loan and investment portfolios came from on high, as when Robert Rubin
persuaded the rest of the senior management of
Citigroup to increase the company's return by taking more risk. In a well-managed company (no one
thinks Citigroup well managed), push-back from
below would be encouraged—from brilliant analysts more knowledgeable than senior managers
about the limitations of the impressive mathematical tools of risk management. My point is only that
problems of communication and control are en-
demic to organizations, especially large ones, and
played a role in the crisis.

The emergence of the organizational problems
that I have mentioned coincided with the creation
of the new financial instruments—the mortgage-
backed securities and credit-default swaps and
other novel financial instruments that were even
more complex. Organizations stressed by rapid
expansion were further stressed by the analytical
challenges posed by the new instruments, just
as the financial institutions of the 1920s had been
stressed by the new financial methods of that era,
such as installment buying by consumers and bank
lending to buyers of stock on margin. Organizational problems (another one is the tendency I

mentioned to weight the advice of traders more heavily than that of risk managers) increase the likelihood of mistakes. But they are problems to avoid or solve; they do not signify irrationality.

Emotion does play a role in the behavior of businessmen and consumers, as of all human beings, but it is not necessarily or even typically irrational. It is a form of telescoped thinking, like intuition, and often it is superior to conscious analytic procedures. A driver who swerves in alarm to avoid hitting a pedestrian is not irrational because he failed to conduct a cost-benefit analysis before swerving. Many of the examples given to show that financial behavior is irrational are superficial—for example that many people buy stocks at the peak of the market and sell at the trough, when they should be doing the reverse. There would not be a peak without buyers or a trough without sellers. No one knows when a market has peaked; until that happens prices are rising, and even in a bubble (but one is never certain it *is* a bubble) it is a fair guess that they will continue to rise for a time. No one knows when stock prices have reached their bottom, either, and it may be prudent to sell at a loss in a down market in order to eliminate the risk of a larger loss if stocks continue to decline. Because people have different expectations and different attitudes toward bearing risk, there are gains from trade along a broad spectrum of possible stock prices.

Of course it is dumb to expect every trend to continue indefinitely, as the influential school of economic thought known as "rational expectations" has reminded us. But in settings of profound uncertainty it may be impossible to do better than to assume that tomorrow will be like today. Business uncertainty has a further significance that is brought out in Keynes's statement (in *The General Theory*, pp. 162–163) "that human decisions affecting the future, whether personal or political or economic, cannot depend on strict mathematical expectation, since the basis for making such calculations does not exist; and that it is our innate urge to activity which makes the wheels go round, our rational selves choosing between the alternatives as best we are able, calculating where we can, but often falling back for our motive on whim or sentiment or chance."

A choice under profound uncertainty is not adding a column of numbers but firing a shot in the dark, and so we should consider the character traits (not character flaws) that make some people willing to act on such a basis. They will be people who have a below-average aversion to uncertainty and, since we are speaking of business, an above-average love of making money. They were bound to swarm into financial intermediation in the era created by Alan Greenspan's monetary policy that offered prospects of great wealth to smart people willing to take large risks. Such people are not irrational, but their clustering in financial intermediation when the wraps are taken off risky lending enhances the inherent instability of that business.

Similarly, it is not irrational, though often thought to be, to allow oneself to be influenced by what other people are doing. You may doubt that the price of some tradable asset will continue to rise, but the fact that it is rising means that other people disagree with you. They may know something you don't. Often they do. It is risky but not irrational to follow the herd. (It is also risky to abandon the safety of the herd—ask any wildebeest.) That is why buying a stock because others are buying it and thus forcing up its price is not irrational. And likewise while it can be very dangerous to be a prisoner of your preconceptions, as I will note in discussing the role of ideology in the failure of government officials and economics professors alike to have anticipated and responded effectively to the depression, it is irrational to think without preconceptions, because preconceptions impound vital knowledge as well as prejudice.

These examples suggest that the line between the rational and the irrational is at best unclear, and this is one reason for not placing much weight on the irrational aspects of economic behavior. A more important reason is that the current depression can be explained without hypothesizing irrationality, though not without assuming a certain amount of randomness (fortuity, "bad luck"). Begin with the bubble, or rather bubbles (housing and credit). An asset-price bubble sounds like something irrational. With fundamentals of demand and supply unchanged, the prices of some class of assets skyrocket and then collapse. Actually bubbles tend to be rational responses to uncertainty about the possible effects of a major innovation. In the 1920s, with the rapid growth of productivity in manufacturing and the development of new methods of borrowing, there was reason to believe that the nation had entered a long era of rapid, sustained economic growth. Suppose investors were properly sober—they thought the nation *might* be at such a threshold, not that it *was*. Still, uncertainty increases the expected value of a company's stock, particularly a new company's, because the sky is the limit to the value the stock may attain (think of Google) but the potential loss is cut off at zero. (This asymmetry is the unintended consequence of limited corporate liability—that is, of the fact that shareholders cannot be sued for the losses of the corporation.) So go for it—reach for the stars.

The same thing was true in the 1990s, with the revolution in information technology, widely heralded as the beginning of a new era, and again there was a stock bubble. The housing and credit bubbles of the 2000s were a response to what seemed a new era in finance as a result of the widespread securitization of debt and a global capital surplus that was expected to keep interest rates low indefinitely—the Federal Reserve having been thought to have discovered how to keep interest rates low without spawning inflation.

In each era the bubble began as a sensible bet on a bright though uncertain future; it continued to expand, even as fears began to be voiced that it might indeed be a bubble (that is, that the rising price did not reflect a change in fundamentals); and it burst when the market realized that the expectation of a new era had once again been mistaken (or perhaps had been perceived prematurely). At no stage need irrationality be posited to explain what happened. Leverage increases risk, but it also increases expected return, and it is not irrational to accept that tradeoff within limits that in the latest bubbles were not thought to have been exceeded, because of the new financial instruments that were believed to minimize risk. Indeed they, along with the magical combination of low interest rates with low inflation, were the key innovations that made the era seem new, along with one I haven't mentioned yet—the special investment vehicle. A bank that created a risky asset, say some form of collateralized debt obligation (a more complicated version of a mortgage-backed security), might place it in a separate entity, created to hold the asset, rather than keeping it on its books, so that if the asset crashed the bank's capital would not be impaired. As long as the bank disclosed in advance that it was not guaranteeing any losses sustained by the entity, investors could not complain; they would be taking a risk with their eyes wide open. The special investment vehicle was thus another device for parceling out risk in accordance with the risk preferences or aversions of particular investors.

The enormous returns that financial firms can make by borrowing heavily when interest rates are very low and lending into an expanding market provided a rational incentive for a firm to increase its leverage to a point at which bankruptcy was a non-negligible, though small, perceived risk. Formally, a rational firm will increase its leverage to the point at which a further increase would add more to the expected costs of bankruptcy (the costs of bankruptcy to the firm's managers and share-holders—for those would be the costs that mattered to senior management—multiplied by its probability) than to the firm's expected profits. Stated differently, a rational firm will insure (as by reducing its leverage) against the risk of bankruptcy only up to the point at which the cost of insurance, for example in reduced profits, is less than the expected cost of bankruptcy.

Especially when interest rates are low, riding a bubble can be rational even though you know it's a bubble. For you can't know when it will burst, and until it does it is expanding and that means that values are rising rapidly, so that if you climb off the bubble you will have forgone a large profit opportunity. As Citigroup's then CEO put it in July 2007, "When the music stops, in terms of liquidity, things will be complicated. But as long as the music is playing, you've got to get up and dance. We're still dancing." (He didn't know it, but the music had stopped.) And we'll see shortly that even if you know you're riding a bubble *and* are scared to be doing so, it is difficult to climb off without paying a big price.

"Even if you *know* you're riding a bubble . . ." But how do you know until it bursts? It is difficult to second-guess the market—to say that stock prices are too high because they've risen to a level at which the ratio of companies' earnings to the price of their stock is ridiculously high, or that a 20 percent jump in housing prices in one year is excessive because wealth, population, and construction costs do not increase by so much in a year. It is true that during what we *now* know was a housing bubble the ratio of home prices to rentals rose, suggesting that people were indeed speculating in houses—otherwise the ratio should have remained unchanged because residential ownership and rental are close substitutes. But one must own a house to speculate in the housing market, and speculation is a valid method of aligning prices with underlying values. We now know that the rise in prices was a bubble because prices didn't just stop rising; they stopped and then fell sharply, and no change in fundamental values could be found to explain either the steep rise or the steep fall. But before the fall the existence of a bubble could only be suspected, not confirmed. Ben Bernanke, the current chairman of the Federal Reserve, whom no one thinks prone to "irrational exuberance," said in the fall of 2005 (when he was chairman of the President's Council of Economic Advisers)—just as the bubble was about to burst—that the rise in housing prices was *not* a bubble, that rather it was the result, at least primarily, of changes in fundamental economic forces affecting the housing industry.

As for the difficulty of climbing down off a bubble even if you recognize it as such, suppose a bank's management tells its investors, "We're afraid we're riding a housing bubble by being heavily invested in mortgage-backed securities, and because we fear that the bubble may burst soon we are going to reduce our leverage or place more of our capital in less risky assets and this means that your short-run return will be less. But we think that in the long run you'll be better off, although we cannot be certain of that and we do not know how long you'll have to wait." As long as the other banks are continuing to ride the bubble, this will be a hard sell. Your investors, observing that the investors in your competitors are continuing to make a lot of money, are apt to think you're simply offering an excuse for failure. Moreover, investors can lower their risk by diversifying their portfolios, so the fact that they own stock in some firms that have a very high ratio of fixed to variable costs and are therefore at risk of bankruptcy needn't worry them.

One might think a bubble would collapse before it got too big because investors who realized it was a bubble would sell short—in this case, sell interests in mortgage-backed securities short. But short selling in a bubble is very risky unless the bubble is expected to burst very soon. A short seller typically borrows securities that he thinks will lose value and contracts to sell them at a specified price (presumably close to the current market price) on a specified future date. If the market price has fallen by then, he buys the identical securities at that lower price and returns them to the lender. If his prediction of the future price is wrong and the price of the securities is higher when the date for the delivery of the securities he has sold arrives, he will lose money, because he will be paying more for the shares that he returns to the lender than he got for selling the identical number of shares. And he can lose big, because there is no ceiling on the possible increase in the price of a stock. If you buy a stock for $10 and it crashes, still the crash can't cost you more than $10. But if you agree to sell a stock for $10 and when it comes time for you to deliver it (you have to buy it in order to be able to deliver it) its price has risen to $100, you have lost $90, whereas if you buy there is no definite limit to how well you can do. As Keynes put it, "The market can stay irrational longer than you can stay solvent."

It may seem puzzling that banks continued to make risky loans after the housing bubble burst in 2006. But there was still plenty of demand for loans because interest rates remained low. Banks that acknowledged the shakiness of their mortgage-backed securities and hence the thinness of their equity cushion would have had to curtail lending, and their profits would have suffered. There was also a musical-chairs problem. Banks originated mortgage-backed securities as well as buying and selling them, and if an originating bank could find a buyer quickly the sale would shift the risk to him. The crash happened so fast that many originators had not yet sold their mortgage-backed securities and so were stuck holding a rapidly depreciating asset. So a credit bubble succeeded the housing bubble and began leaking air about a year after the housing bubble burst.

The tendency of corporate management to cling to a bubble and hope for the best—or, equivalently, the tendency to maximize short-run profits—is strengthened if, as on Wall Street during the boom, executive compensation is both very generous and truncated on the downside. For then every day that you stay in you make a lot of money, and you know that when the bubble bursts you'll be okay because you have negotiated a generous severance package with your board of directors. Limited liability is a factor too; neither an executive heavily invested in his company's stock nor any other shareholder will be personally liable for the company's losses should it go broke.

And how do executives get such a sweet deal? Well, the board will have hired a compensation consultant who will have advised generosity in fixing the compensation of senior management and as part of that largesse will have recommended that senior executives receive a fat severance package (a "golden parachute") if they are terminated. The consultant will have told the board this because if the board is generous to senior management, senior management may out of gratitude hire the consultant to do other consulting for the firm. And the board will have listened to the consultant's recommendation because the board will have been predisposed to be generous with senior executives' salaries. Most members of a corporation's board of directors will be senior executives themselves. And because a firm's chief executive officer has a say in whether board members are reelected to the board, the higher a board member thinks CEO compensation should be, the more boards he will be invited to join.

So board members have a conflict of interest when it comes to setting executive compensation, and that is not the only pertinent conflict of interest at work in the financial industry. Legislators who receive big campaign contributions from banks have an incentive to favor weak banking regulation, as otherwise those contributions will dwindle. And accountants, since they are paid by the firms they audit, are reluctant to flag their clients' default risks. Granted, often those risks are not disclosed in the documents that accountants review in conducting an audit, but sometimes they are.

The more generous an executive's compensation and the more insulated his compensation package is from any adversity that may befall his company, the greater will be his incentive to maximize profits in the short run—especially in a bubble, where the short run is highly profitable but the long run a looming disaster. His incentive will be even greater if it is a housing bubble. A risky mortgage will carry a high interest rate in order to compensate the mortgagee (or the purchaser of a security backed by the mortgage) for bearing the risk of default. But because defaults will be spread out over the life of the loan, the high interest rate will be sure to generate a high profit initially. Only later will defaults erode that profit. And remember that the issuer of the security will receive his fee for securitization up front, before there is time for many defaults of mortgages that back the security to have occurred.

The incentive to maximize profits in the short run is especially great for a firm's traders, as distinct from its senior management. Consider the following example (based on a recent paper by Dean Foster and Peyton Young). A trader is given $100 million to play with. He invests it in Treasury notes that pay 3 percent interest and, for a $7 million annual fee, sells $100 million in credit insurance against an event that has a 7 percent annual probability of occurring. The sum of the fee and interest is $10 million, which represents a 10 percent annual return on his investment. The probability that he will have to cough up $100 million to the insurer within five years is only 30 percent $(1 - (1 - .93)^5)$, and if the event insured against does not occur within that period he will have been paid handsomely for generating such a high return on the investment. In fact he is taking a high risk, and the firm's risk managers will probably stop him. But the example is a very simple one, and the trader—who, remember, is likely to have greater influence with his superiors than a risk manager—will try to make the transaction as complicated as possible.

And if a firm realizes that because of risky investments disaster is looming, we may observe "gambling for resurrection." If management has a choice between bankruptcy in six months, a safe investment that will postpone bankruptcy for eight months, and a risky investment that carries an 80 percent probability of bankruptcy in one month and a 20 percent probability that the firm will avoid bankruptcy altogether, the last choice may well be the one most attractive to management even though it is the riskiest. That is one reason a bubble may collapse with terrifying rapidity, as happened with the credit bubble in September 2008.

The incentive of corporate executives to maximize short-run profits in a bubble situation can be held in check by backloading executive compensation (the opposite of a severance benefit), for example by giving them, instead of cash, company stock that they are forbidden to sell for a significant period of time. (The severance package hedges the executives against the full negative consequences to them of making the company as risky as the shareholders want.) Companies do that, but often insufficiently to deflect their executives from excessive focus on the short run.

Before the financial crisis, much of the economic literature on executive compensation argued that corporate executives should be pushed to take *more* risk than they would like to. The more an executive's compensation depends on how well his firm does, the fewer risks he may be inclined to take, because all or most of his financial eggs, as distinct from the shareholders', are in that one basket. That is why asymmetric compensation schemes in which compensation tied to stock value is combined with a generous severance package may be in investors' interest. But such schemes may not be in the interest of the nation as a whole if they enhance the risk of a depression—and they do.

Securitization also played a role in encouraging short-term profit maximization. Instead of having to wait twenty-five or thirty years to receive the full return on a residential mortgage, exchanging the mortgage for a security gave a bank the present value of the loan up front, increasing the bank's current profits, some part of which would accrue to the bank's executives in the form of salary, bonus, benefits, or stock. A bank could always have sold a mortgage, but securitization made the mortgage market more liquid.

I am not suggesting that executives, especially at the highest level of a major company, seek to maximize their current income knowing that in a year or two the company will go broke and they will be fired. With or without explicit backloading of compensation, CEOs tend to be heavily invested in stock of their firm. Senior management in firms like Lehman Brothers and Bear Stearns lost heavily when their firms went belly-up. But the greater the gains are from taking risks that enable very high short-term profits, and the better cushioned the executive is by his severance package against the cost of losing his job, the more risks he rationally will take.

And recall the earlier point that financial catastrophes, like other types of catastrophe, tend to be rare events. Managers have a limited time horizon. This gives them an incentive to take risks that are small in terms of probability even if, should one of the risks materialize, the result would be disaster; for the disaster is unlikely to occur during the tenure of the current managers.

A final reason for executives' not trying to peer too far into the future in making business decisions is that, as with the weather, accurate long-term forecasting of business values is impossible. Maybe it's sensible therefore for businessmen, especially in financial markets, which are notably volatile, to focus on the near term. But that makes it harder for them to avoid bubbles.

Although my focus in discussing managerial conflicts of interest has been on the management of publicly held firms, the analysis applies to private companies, such as most hedge funds and most private equity funds as well, though with diminished force. These are organizations too, albeit less elephantine and therefore less plagued by conflicts between owners and managers. And in fact they have not done as badly in the downturn as the large, publicly held financial firms have done. That is some evidence that the incentive to take risks that is created by executive overcompensation in publicly held companies has been a factor in the financial crisis.

Generous compensation was not limited to the senior management level, but extended to the lower-level executives who made most of the actual investment decisions. The only plausible explanation is that the firms were competing for highly talented analysts and traders, and this is evidence that the crumpling of the banking industry was the result of systemic factors rather than, as the media increasingly are suggesting, stupidity.

Notice that I have listed no psychological factors among the underlying causes of the depression. My narrative has been of intelligent businessmen rationally responding to their environment yet by doing so creating the preconditions for a terrible crash. Readers may be inclined to object that it was the housing bubble, which started the slide toward depression, that was irrational; people should have known better than to take out 100 percent mortgages with adjustable interest rates, and mortgage brokers and mortgage originators should have run more careful credit checks. Had everyone acted prudently, home prices would not have outrun value, soaring in a speculative frenzy.

But not only did real estate brokers, mortgage brokers, and mortgagees do very well for a number of years; so did the mortgagors (the borrowers). And to the extent that the ignorance of home buyers played a role in the housing bubble, as undoubtedly it did, this just means that information is costly. Because it is costly, markets do not always provide enough information to enable consumers to make the "right" decisions, in the sense of the decisions they would have made with full information.

We should distinguish, moreover, between two common types of risky behavior by people who pledge their house as security for a loan. In the first, a homeowner takes out a home equity loan (a loan secured by the borrower's home and thus equivalent to a mortgage) in order to have more money for consumption. By doing this he dissaves and thus increases the risk of default and going broke and getting a lousy credit rating, and perhaps he does not appreciate the risk because he is financially unsophisticated and cannot depend on the lender for candid warnings about the likelihood and consequences of a default. But I am guessing that in most cases he has at least a rough idea of the risk and is quite willing to chance it. There is nothing irrational about stretching to buy a house in a neighborhood with good schools so that your kids can get a better education. I would not expect the cognitive quirks that have been shown to influence the stock market to be as significant when a person is deciding whether or how much money to borrow, and on what terms, though fraud and simple ignorance are doubtless factors.

In the second type of risky home-buying behavior, a person who currently rents rather than owns his residence and has poor credit buys a house with little or no down payment and a fat mortgage with an adjustable interest rate—perhaps it is fixed for the first two years at a below-market level and will be reset at the market level at the end of that period. If the value of the home rises, the buyer's equity in the home will increase, reducing the lender's risk. Suppose the buyer paid $500,000 with a 100 percent mortgage and two years later the house is worth $750,000. The mortgage will now be equal to only two thirds of the value of the house—actually even less if the buyer has paid back some of the principal during those two years. The reduction in the lender's risk brought about by the borrower's having acquired an equity interest in the house, cushioning the lender against loss if there is a default (and default is now less likely), will cause the interest rate to be reset at an affordable level or enable the homeowner to refinance the mortgage at an affordable level; in either event he will have made a successful investment.

If instead the value of the house remains flat or declines, the owner can abandon it and return to rental housing. It is true that he will owe the unpaid balance of the loan, and this means in most states that the mortgagee will be able to obtain a deficiency judgment against him for that balance minus the proceeds of the foreclosure sale. (The "deficiency" is the difference between what the mortgagor owes and what the foreclosure sale yields the mortgagee.) Unless the mortgagor is rich, however, the mortgagee is unlikely to bother to sue him, because litigation is expensive and water cannot be squeezed out of a stone. It is also true that the defaulting mortgagor will get a bad credit rating, but so what? Even people with good credit ratings find it tough to borrow in a depression and anyway may not want to, because they are trying to rebuild their savings. And someone who owes more on his mortgage than his house is worth is unlikely to have a good credit rating anyway. Thus the downside of the home buyer's speculative investment is truncated, making his "reckless" behavior not only rational but also consistent with his being well informed about the risks. In some states, moreover, notably California, the mortgagee cannot obtain a deficiency judgment against a defaulting mortgagor; the mortgage loan is "nonrecourse." So the defaulting mortgagor doesn't have to worry about being sued.

This analysis, while acquitting many subprime and Alt-A mortgagors of irrationality, does help to explain how a rise in housing prices became a bubble. Buying a house that one can afford only if its market value rises before the interest rate is reset at the market level implies that if that value does not rise, even if it doesn't fall either, the buyer is likely to default when the interest rate is reset unless he expects the mortgagee to seek a deficiency judgment against him. The price level will stop rising at some point, and when it does there will be many defaults because many homes will no longer have a positive value for their owners. Those homes will be put up for sale, whether a voluntary sale by the owner or a foreclosure sale. The rash of offers of sale will create a housing glut that pushes down housing prices, triggering more defaults and so a further reduction in prices. By the end of 2008, the average price of a house in the United States was almost 30 percent below what it had been three years earlier.

The culprit is cheap credit rather than irrational behavior by business or consumers. Cheap credit stimulates economic activity, causing asset prices to rise, including the prices of residential real estate, which is a huge part of the nation's asset base. To take advantage of these rising prices, would-be buyers borrow more, so lenders lend more and prices are driven still higher, and lenders borrow more so that they *can* lend more. Leverage tends to rise and the rapid expansion of the banking industry causes strains. At some point the asset-price increase becomes unsustainable, but no one will know in advance what that point is, and there is rational reluctance to forgo lucrative profit opportunities by bailing out before one senses that the plateau (followed by the inevitable crash) is about to be reached. This pattern has been repeated time and again and in country after country.

The usual result is just a recession. But the combination of a dearth of safe savings with a banking industry that is highly leveraged can turn a recession into a depression. When, as a result of heavy losses caused by excessive leverage, the industry pulls back from lending, consumers will have great difficulty borrowing to maintain their consumption, and a steep fall in personal consumption expenditures can tip the economy into deflation by precipitating deep price discounts. Remember that falling prices encourage cash hoarding, which reduces consumption both directly and by reducing lending, since what is hoarded is not lent.

The lower interest rates are, the less one earns from investing in low-risk securities and the cheaper it is to borrow, making it *much* cheaper to borrow and to invest the borrowed money in the stock market or the bubbling housing market. But one is setting oneself up for a fall when asset prices drop.

Risky behavior of the sort I have been describing was individually rational during the bubble. But it was collectively irrational. In deciding to reduce his savings, a person will not consider the negligible effect of his decision on the economy as a whole, any more than a banker will in deciding how high to crank up the leverage in his bank's capital structure. Rational indifference to the indirect consequences of one's business and consumption behavior is the reason the government has a duty, in regulating financial behavior, to do more than prevent fraud, theft, and other infringements of property and contract rights, which is the only duty that libertarians believe government has. Without stronger financial regulation than that, the rational behavior of law-abiding financiers and consumers can precipitate an economic disaster.

Not only does competition force businessmen to be profit maximizers, which implies, as we have seen, that they will accept a small risk of bankruptcy; we *want* them to be profit maximizers—it is what drives economic progress. But in this example private virtue is a public vice, because the profit-maximizing businessman rationally ignores small probabilities that his conduct in conjunction with that of his competitors may bring down the entire economy. Similarly, when the economy is weak, it is rational for people to reduce their consumption and increase their savings. It is the rational response to an economic downturn. But by doing this they make the downturn worse. From an overall social standpoint, we want people to save when times are good and spend when times are bad, but from the individual's standpoint it makes more sense to do the opposite unless one happens to be doing well in bad times or badly in good times. The contrast between private virtue and public vice is especially striking in people who today are curtailing the purchase of luxury items in order to exhibit and inspire frugality. That is a fine gesture from the standpoint of private morality, but if enough people make it the result will be to deepen the depression by significantly reducing personal consumption expenditures.

These examples illustrate the useful economic term "externality." An external cost is a cost imposed by one person on another or others with whom he has no actual or potential contractual relationship. Because of the absence of such a relationship, he does not bear the cost and so is unlikely to give it much weight in deciding what to do—especially if his action creates a significant externality only in conjunction with similar actions of many other people. That is the situation of the individual consumer who desires to plume himself on his frugality by reducing the purchase of luxury items that he can well afford, and of the businessman who decides to take less risk than is profit maximizing in order to benefit the economy as a whole.

Still another reason for the epidemic of dissaving that preceded the crash was rapid advances in marketing sophistication and technology. The World Wide Web played a role here (think how easy one-click ordering makes the buying of consumer products), along with advances in cognitive psychology. Increased sophistication in the marketing of goods and services enabled sellers to induce consumers to shift much of their savings, designed to protect their future consumption, into buying more consumer goods now.

The story of modernity, as Max Weber explained a century ago, is the bringing of more and more activities under the rule of rationality. It is illustrated by the increasing professionalization of activities—ranging from medical care, inventory control, and dating to political campaigning and (other) forms of selling—that used to be hit-or-miss affairs. Professionalized marketing makes people *want* to buy goods and services now rather than save money to buy them in the future—to buy a house now, for example, by borrowing most of the purchase price rather than waiting to buy it until one has saved up the price, which would mean deferring to the distant future the enjoyment of the delights of homeownership. Opening people's eyes to the full range of products that might make them happier is a major economic activity in a commercial society. The economist Frank Knight used to say that the greatest poverty was the poverty not of goods but of wants. That poverty, at least, has been abolished in the United States.

Keynes in *The General Theory* (p. 108) amusingly contrasted six motives for consumption—"Enjoyment, Shortsightedness, Generosity, Miscalculation, Ostentation and Extravagance"—with eight motives for saving: "Precaution, Foresight, Calculation, Improvement, Independence, Enterprise, Pride and Avarice." Marketers to Americans (as distinct from Japanese) have had greater success appealing to the first set of motives than to the second.

Quantitative models of risk—another fulfillment of Weber's prophecy that more and more activities would be brought under the rule of rationality—are also being blamed for the financial crisis. Suppose a trader is contemplating the purchase of a stock using largely borrowed money, so that if the stock falls even a little way the loss will be great. He might consult a statistical model that predicted, on the basis of the ups and downs of the stock in the preceding two years, the probability distribution of the stock's behavior over the next few days or weeks. The criticism is that the model would have based the prediction on market behavior during a period of rising stock values; the modeler should have gone back to the 1980s or earlier to get a fuller picture of the riskiness of the stock. But that might not be helpful. The further back in time one reaches, the less predictive value the behavior of a stock is apt to have, because the company and the economic environment will have changed a lot. The models assumed that the near future would be much like the near past rather than like 1929 or 1987, and the assumption was usually correct and so the models were useful. No quantitative model was going to predict a depression; the data on which such a prediction would be worth anything had not been obtained. It was the failure (which I discuss in the next chapter) to heed warning signs and thus search out the necessary data, rather than a failure of model design, that caused the failure of prediction. And it was a failure of government and of the economics profession rather than of business, as business foresight is rationally truncated, as I have argued.

In sum, rational maximization by businessmen and consumers, all pursuing their self-interest more or less intelligently within a framework of property and contract rights, can set the stage for an economic catastrophe. There is no need to bring cognitive quirks, emotional forces, or character flaws into the causal analysis. This is important both in simplifying analysis and in avoiding a search, likely to be futile, for means by which government can alter the mentality or character of businessmen and consumers.

The essential point is the difference between a 1 percent probability that a firm will go broke, because of risky lending, and a 1 percent probability of a depression because the leading financial firms have a correlated 1 percent risk of going broke. The toleration of the risk is rational for each firm, irrational for society.

Conservatives do not agree that the economic emergency is a failure of the market to internalize the costs of an economy-wide catastrophe. They argue that the cause was government. They point to legislative pressures on banks to facilitate homeownership by easing mortgage requirements and conditions, to which could be added the deductibility of mortgage interest payments and interest on home equity loans, along with real estate taxes, from taxable income and the repeal in 1997 of capital gains tax on most resales of residential property.

I examine some of the legislative pressures later. For now it is enough to note that small-government conservatives, at least those who were in power, were happy with these policies—President Bush pushed homeownership as a cornerstone of the "ownership society" that he advocated as part of his political philosophy of "compassionate conservatism"—until a governmental scapegoat was needed to explain the depression.

The housing bubble and the risky lending practices could have been prevented by more aggressive regulation and the elimination of tax benefits for homeowners. But the absence of these or other preventive measures was the result not of too much government but of too little: not of intrusive, heavy-handed regulation of housing and finance but of deregulation, hostility to taxation and to government in general, and a general laissez-faire attitude, "conservative" in a currently prevailing sense of the word. Conservatives wanted taxes to be lower rather than higher and regulation to be lighter. They considered markets to be self-regulating, from which it followed that bubbles, risky lending, defaults, and other market perturbations would be self-correcting unless the government interfered. (In an older sense of "conservative," risky lending, risky borrowing, heavy indebtedness, bubbles, and speculation would have been thought antithetical to a conservatively managed economy.)

There is an illuminating analogy to industrial pollution in capitalist society. Suppose government provides no remedies at all (whether judicial or administrative) against harms from pollution. Then rational profit-maximizing producers, in deciding how much to pollute, will not consider the effects of their pollution on people with whom they have no actual or potential contractual relationship (as they do with their workers). Yet when those effects are taken into consideration the social costs of the pollution may exceed the cost savings from not doing anything about it.

If government refused to do anything about pollution, one could call its refusal a "cause" of the pollution if one wanted, but a more illuminating formulation would be that the government had failed to do anything about pollution caused by industry. Similarly, the social costs of a recession or depression are external to the rational self-interested decision-making of financial institutions because nothing an individual firm can do will avert such an event. The aggregate self-interested decisions of these institutions produce the economic crisis by a kind of domino effect that only government can prevent—which it failed to do. That was a grave government failure, which allowed a failure of the financial market to produce disastrous consequences for society as a whole.

The roots of the failure lay in widespread dissatisfaction, beginning in the 1970s, with public-utility and common-carrier regulation, and other forms of economic regulation as well, including the regulation of banking and investment. The economists who inspired the deregulation movement were not macroeconomists and did not differentiate between banking and other regulated industries, such as railroads and airlines. They were not alert to the macroeconomic implications of competition in banking; and macroeconomists, as we shall see, thought that the problem of depressions had been solved.

We must not ignore the costs of regulation. Some market failures cannot be corrected at a cost less than the social cost of the market failure, and it is best to ignore them. But are depressions such a market failure? They are not, even if we could be confident that a depression would occur only once every eighty years (this year is the eightieth anniversary of the stock market crash of October 1929), and of course we cannot be. The Great Depression of the 1930s inflicted horrendous costs, quite apart from the suffering inflicted on tens of millions of Americans, not to mention—since it was a global depression—more tens of millions abroad. Among the costs, as conservatives should take note, were the excesses of the New Deal. And without the depression there might have been no Nazi Germany and no World War II. The costs of the present depression may include a swing to excessive regulation, a politically as well as economically unhealthy dependence of business on government largesse (I give an example later, involving Citigroup), a huge loss of economic output, an immense increase in the national debt, a high inflation rate, a decline in U.S. world economic power, a weakening of the nation's geopolitical power as the country turns inward to address its economic problems, and increased political instability in many parts of the world. It may turn out that if the asset-price bubbles of the last decade are subtracted from measures of economic growth, the U.S. economy will be adjudged to have been stagnant—that rather than being productive during this period, Americans were living on borrowed money.

4

Why a Depression Was Not Anticipated

AN ARTICLE on the front page of the business section of the *New York Times* of October 11, 2008, attributed the almost universal failure to anticipate the financial crisis (certainly to anticipate its gravity) to "insanity"—more precisely, to a psychological inability to give proper weight to past events, so that if there is prosperity today people assume it will last forever even though they know that in the past booms have always been followed by busts. For many people in many of life's settings, the best predictive method is to assume that the future, especially the near future, will resemble the past, especially the recent past. I remember when the best method of forecasting tomorrow's weather was to assume it would be like today's.

But it seems unlikely that such experts on the business cycle as the Federal Reserve's chairman, Ben Bernanke, are constrained to base their predictions on naïve extrapolation. This makes his neglect, and that of other experts both inside and outside the government, of warning signs of a coming crash extremely puzzling. Real estate bubbles are common. The supply of "good" land is fixed in the short run, the housing stock is extremely durable and therefore does not expand rapidly when demand increases, and land and the improvements on it cannot be sold short. And the bursting of a real estate bubble can lead to bank insolvencies—has done so in the past, as in Japan in the late 1980s and other East Asian countries in the 1990s—because most real estate has heavy indebtedness and real estate debt is a significant fraction of all debt. Hence the dependence of banking on real estate, and hence how a nationwide collapse of housing values can carry the banking industry down with it. Our real estate bubbles had been local before this one, but there was no reason to think we couldn't experience a nationwide real estate bubble. The Federal Reserve's insouciance about the danger of such a bubble is a mystery.

I said you never *know* you're in a bubble until it bursts. But when the rise in housing prices began to show signs of slowing in 2005 after having risen more than 60 percent since 2000, talk about a housing bubble in the general media—the financial journals, as we know, had been far ahead—started in earnest. Newspaper articles featured such headlines as "Housing Bubble Is Real, So Don't Get Hurt When It Finally Pops," "If Housing Bubble Pops, Look Out!," "Hear a Pop? Watch Out," "Economists: Housing Boom Could Lead to Busts," "Four Out of 10 Americans Fear Real-Estate Bubble," "Efforts to Regulate Risky Mortgage Innovations Are So Far Ignored," and "Risky Lending Spurs 'Bubble.'" There was an especially prescient editorial entitled "Risky Mortgage Business" in the *New York Times* of July 6, 2005. Yet in October 2005, Bernanke denied there was a housing bubble, saying that "these price increases largely reflect strong economic fundamentals." One of the "fundamentals" he mentioned was that the supply of land is limited; and the less elastic (that is, readily expandable) supply is, the bigger the effect on price of a rise in demand. True; but housing prices rose steeply in areas of Arizona, California, Florida, and Nevada in which land for home building was plentiful. That was evidence of a bubble. Bernanke's understanding of the housing market was incomplete.

The alarm bells were sounded ever more loudly

in 2006, 2007, and the first six months of 2008. But the financial crisis when it finally struck the nation full-blown in September 2008 surprised the government, the financial community, the economics profession, and the public, even though it had been building for three years.

The Federal Reserve began to worry a little about housing prices in 2006, and it raised the federal funds rate in that and the following year. That is the interest rate at which banks borrow reserves from each other. It influences other interest rates because banks' ability to make loans is, as we know, limited by their reserves. The higher the federal funds rate, the more costly it is for a bank to respond to a loan request by borrowing reserves from another bank. The added cost drives up interest rates, though a complication is that the federal funds rate is a short-term interest rate and long-term rates sometimes follow their own path.

The federal funds rate was raised to 5.25 percent in June 2006. (It is now between zero percent and a quarter of 1 percent, as the Fed desperately endeavors to induce lending. A zero federal funds rate means that the price of reserves is zero.) The goal, however, was not to reduce credit transactions as such but to avert inflation. Interest rates on mortgages, which are long-term rates, were not greatly affected. The Federal Reserve could have raised the commercial banks' reserve requirements to limit lending, or sold federal securities to them. Either measure would have constrained their lending further, the first because reserves are not available for lending and the second because when the Fed sells securities to a bank and retires the cash it receives from the sale there is that much less money available for the bank to lend. The Federal Reserve did neither of these things. Interest rates on mortgages did increase some, as an indirect result of the raising of the federal funds rate, and the increase was probably a factor in the bursting of the housing bubble. Yet as late as August 2007 the Federal Reserve was predicting sustained economic expansion and expressed concern only about inflation in the sense of an increase in the consumer price index.

Beginning in September 2007, with concerns about inflation giving way to concerns about a possible recession, the Federal Reserve began reducing the federal funds rate and making some additional credit available to banks; and early in 2008 Congress enacted a modest ($168 billion) tax-rebate bill. These measures were too little and too late. They reflected fear of a mild recession, tempered by anxiety about inflation; they did not reflect fear of a full-blown financial crisis that could trigger a depression. The Federal Reserve should have raised interest rates sooner, to prick the housing bubble, and lowered them sooner, to prevent the banking collapse. Yet Allan Meltzer, a well-known macroeconomist, in an interview in April 2008 criticized Bernanke's reduction of interest rates, calling it "a silly policy designed to head off a recession that may come but hasn't come yet." And the Federal Reserve did not reduce the federal funds rate between June 2008 and mid-September, when the banks collapsed; it was again worrying about inflation.

We can get help in understanding the blindness of experts to warning signs from the literature on surprise attacks, such as Roberta Wohlstetter's book *Pearl Harbor: Warning and Decision* (1962). As Wohlstetter explains, there were many warnings in 1941 that Japan was going to attack Western possessions in Southeast Asia, such as the oil-rich Dutch East Indies (now Indonesia). An attack on the U.S. fleet in Hawaii, known to be within range of Japan's large carrier fleet, would be a logical measure for protecting the eastern flank of a Japanese attack on the Dutch East Indies, Burma, or Malaya.

Among the factors that caused the warnings to be disregarded were prior beliefs (preconceptions), the cost and difficulty of taking effective defensive measures against an uncertain danger, and the absence of a mechanism for aggregating, sifting, and analyzing warning information flowing in from many sources and for pushing it up to the decision-making level of government. Most informed observers in 1941 thought that Japan would not attack the United States because it was too weak to have a reasonable chance of winning a war with us; they did not understand Japanese culture, which placed a higher value on honor than on national survival. And securing all possible targets of Japanese aggression against attack would have been immensely costly and a diversion from our preparations for war against Germany, deemed inevitable. Denial of the Japanese menace was a psychologically appealing way of avoiding having to confront the immense difficulty of protecting against Japanese aggression. And there was no Central Intelligence Agency or other institution dedicated to aggregating and analyzing attack warnings.

Similar factors made it difficult to heed the warning signs of the 2008 financial crisis. Although a number of reputable business leaders, economists, and financial reporters had been warning for years that our financial institutions were excessively leveraged, they made little impression on government officials, the stock market, or the public at large. On August 17, 2008 — just a month before the financial tsunami — the *New York Times Magazine* published an article foolishly but revealingly entitled "Dr. Doom" about a reputable academic economist, a professor at New York University named Nouriel Roubini, who for years had been predicting with uncanny accuracy what has now happened. The article reported that in September 2006 — two years before the financial crisis but after the bursting of the housing bubble — Roubini had "announced that a crisis was brewing. In the coming months and years, he warned, the United States was likely to face a once-in-a-lifetime housing bust, an oil shock, sharply declining consumer confidence and, ultimately, a deep recession. He laid out a bleak sequence of events: homeowners defaulting on mortgages, trillions of dollars of mortgage-backed securities unraveling worldwide and the global financial system shuddering to a halt. These developments, he went on, could cripple or destroy hedge funds, investment banks and other major financial institutions like Fannie Mae and Freddie Mac."

Roubini was not the only prophet without honor in his own country. In a March 2006 article in *The Economists' Voice* entitled "The Menace of an Unchecked Housing Bubble," another economist, Dean Baker, had written: "When the downturn in house prices occurs, many homeowners will have mortgages that exceed the value of their homes, a situation that is virtually certain to send default rates soaring. This will put lenders that hold large amounts of mortgage debt at risk, and possibly jeopardize the solvency of Fannie Mae and Freddie Mac, since they guarantee much of this debt. If these mortgage giants faced collapse, a government bailout (similar to the S&L bailout), involving hundreds of billions of dollars, would be virtually inevitable." Baker, like Roubini, had hit the bull's eye. But no one in a position of authority in government, and very few in business, paid any attention, just as no one had paid attention to the warnings sounded years earlier by *The Economist*. A particularly sharp warning against the Federal Reserve's policy of allowing asset-price bubbles to expand in the belief that the consequences could always be handled by flooding the economy with money—a warning that actually invoked the Great Depression—was issued by the prestigious Bank for International Settlements in June 2007; it was ignored too.

There had been many other warnings as well, especially after Bear Stearns' collapse in March 2008, and, almost a year earlier, after two mortgage hedge funds operated by Bear Sterns and three by the French bank BNP Paribas collapsed. The biggest warning sign of all had appeared much earlier—when Long-Term Capital Management faltered in 1998, was taken over by its creditors in a deal arranged by the Federal Reserve, and then expired. LTCM was a highly leveraged hedge fund that as a result of heavy trading in derivatives (securities based on other securities, such as futures contracts, options, and swaps) was entwined with other financial firms all over the world, just like Lehman Brothers. LTCM overestimated the degree to which it had diversified the risks that it took with its investments, and as a result of its mistake lost heavily when Russia's sudden repudiation of its public and private debt caused the value of speculative securities to plummet as investors sought refuge in safe assets.

The fall of LTCM illustrated how risky trading could endanger the entire financial system. Yet because the danger was quickly contained and certain controls on trading in derivatives were instituted voluntarily (such as requiring collateral), the possibility of a repetition, perhaps on a larger scale not so easy to contain, was ignored. The senior economic officials of the Clinton Administration rejected a proposal by the chairwoman of the Commodity Futures Trading Commission, Brooksley Born, to bring the new derivatives under regulation, as some older types of derivative, such as futures contracts, already were. Lawrence Summers, then Deputy Secretary of the Treasury, told Congress that "the parties to these kinds of contract are largely sophisticated financial institutions that would appear to be eminently capable of protecting themselves from fraud *and counterparty insolvencies*" (my emphasis). That turned out not to be true.

The collapse of LTCM is illuminating in another way. Within a matter of months an apparently stable financial network consisting of LTCM and the firms all around the world with which it had contractual relations received a jolt that nearly destroyed it. That should not have been a complete surprise, because an interrelated system of financial intermediaries is inherently unstable. Any firm that borrows short term and lends long term is at risk of a run, and the run and the resulting collapse of the firm may have a domino effect on the lenders to it and the borrowers from it and the financial companies with which they are entwined. If A borrows from B and lends to C, and C defaults, B, fearing the effect on A of C's default, may call its loan, which may cause A to default on its other debts, imperiling those creditors in turn. It might seem that to avoid such risks banks would borrow long term rather than short term. But then they would make less profit on loans. Short-term interest rates are almost always lower than long-term rates; the short-term lender has less risk not only because his money is tied up for a shorter time but also because he has greater liquidity—if he needs cash, he won't have to wait a long time for the loan that he has made to be repaid. He pays for these benefits of short-term lending by accepting a lower interest rate.

Not that borrowing short and lending long is a surefire formula for making money; it is not—which underscores the inherent riskiness of financial intermediation. To the extent that the higher interest rate on a long-term loan is compensation for the increased risk of default, it is a real cost. To make a profit (and cover its other costs), a bank has to be able either to identify potential borrowers who are less likely to default than the market interest rate assumes, or to diversify risk better than other lenders. But the bank's profit from arbitraging the short-term and long-term interest rates is likely to be small—without the use of leverage. Suppose a bank has capital of $1 billion, but only $40 million in equity. Even if the average difference between its borrowing cost and the interest (after adjustment for risk) that it obtains from lending its capital is only 1 percent, 1 percent of $1 billion is $10 million, and this translates into a 25 percent return on equity, though much of that will be eaten up by other costs of doing business besides the borrowing cost. But leverage drives up risk as well as return, and with banks being financially entwined with one another the collapse of one can bring down others in a chain reaction. In the old days, when bank capital was primarily supplied by demand deposits, bank leverage was limited by the requirement still in force that a bank have reserves (cash or cash equivalents) equal to a specified percentage of those deposits. But deposits to which the requirement applies are no longer the major source of banks' capital.

Notice the pernicious effect of competition, and ultimately of deregulation, on bank safety. Deregulation increased competition in banking by allowing other financial firms to offer close substitutes for banking services. Increased competition in turn compressed the margin between the interest rates that banks paid to borrow capital for lending and the interest rates they charged their borrowers. The narrower the margin, the more leverage banks need in order to obtain enough revenue net of their borrowing costs to cover other expenses and provide a return to their shareholders.

Commercial banks used to concentrate on making short-term loans, which they could do profitably because their principal capital consisted of demand deposits that were interest-free. But with deregulation, banks began making loans that did not come due for many years, such as thirty-year residential mortgages. They had no choice. They had to make long-term loans because their deposit capital declined as people and firms switched to money market accounts and firms practiced sweeps; these developments upped the banks' cost of obtaining capital and pushed them to seek a higher yield by lending long term. (Yet banks also derive a benefit from sweeps; sweeps reduce reserve requirements, which are a percentage of the bank's demand deposits, and thus enable banks to lend more.) Other financial intermediaries could borrow short and lend long without regulatory limitations; banks sought and largely obtained the same right.

"Domino effect" is not quite the right metaphor with which to describe the collapse of a financial network. One either leaves a domino alone or gives it a slight push that makes all the other dominos collapse. What happened to LTCM, and in the fall of 2008 to a host of other financial intermediaries, belongs to the domain of chaos theory, illustrated (before "chaos theory" was invented) by Irving Fisher's example of a boat capsizing. As a slight variant, consider leaning while sitting in a canoe. At first it just tilts, but if you keep leaning, all of a sudden the canoe will capsize. Until that moment, hard to gauge in advance, the canoe seems stable; in actuality it is vulnerable to a slight additional exertion of force. The same is true of the financial system, except that it's impossible to calculate the exact conditions that will precipitate collapse, and this uncertainty makes it impossible to predict the collapse with any precision. Hence the limitations of risk management.

I have been repeating much that I said in the preceding chapters, but I have done so in order to make as clear as I can that the concern that Roubini expressed about the fragility of the credit system was solidly grounded in the economics of financial intermediaries and the potentially lethal combination of low interest rates and the deregulation of banking. And if that were not enough, by the time the *Times* article on Roubini appeared, most of his predictions had already come true, yet he continued to be ignored. Until the biggest financial ninepins started falling in September 2008, the magnitude of the crisis was largely invisible to government, the business community, and most economists, even specialists in financial economics and in macroeconomics. Bernanke had declared it unlikely that the mortgage defaults that accelerated after the housing bubble burst would spill over to the financial system or the broader, nonfinancial economy. In May 2007, for example, he said: "Importantly, we see no serious broader spillover to banks or thrift institutions from the problems in the subprime market." Yet by then a great many banks and thrift institutions were insolvent. In February 2008 he said: "I expect there will be some failures," referring to smaller regional banks that had invested heavily in mortgage-backed securities, but that "among the largest banks, the capital ratios remain good and I don't anticipate any serious problems of that sort among the large, internationally active banks that make up a very substantial part of our banking system." Bear Stearns collapsed the next month.

In September, Bernanke and Paulson, between them in full command of American economic policy, let Lehman Brothers fail, apparently without realizing the consequences of the failure—a worldwide credit freeze and a plunge in stock values. Before Lehman Brothers collapsed, it was not even certain that there was a recession; after it collapsed, it was likely that there was going to be a depression. Yet in October, Bernanke and Paulson were still insisting that the banking industry's problem was illiquidity, not insolvency. Not until late in November did the Federal Reserve commit to a lending program commensurate with depression conditions. By then a depression—which might have been headed off six months earlier, at the time of the collapse of Bear Stearns, had the rescues attempted in the fall of 2008 been made then—was inevitable. For bank rescues do not take effect the day they're announced. Producers and consumers who have begun to adjust to the expectation of a serious economic contraction can't go into reverse the minute a rescue is announced; they don't know when it will be implemented and with what conditions and consequences. They *still* don't know.

Why were the warnings and warning signs ignored before it was too late, rather than, if not believed, at least investigated? Preconceptions played a role. It is tempting, indeed irresistible under conditions of uncertainty, to base policy to a degree on theoretical preconceptions, on a worldview, an ideology. Indeed, it would be irrational to be a tabula rasa; it would mean discarding useful knowledge. But preconceptions, shaped as they are by past experiences, can impede reactions to novel challenges. If government officials, and the economists on whom they leaned most heavily, had had less confidence in the resilience of markets, they might have studied the housing and financial markets for warning signs of market failure. But most economists, and the kind of officials who tend to be appointed by Republican Presidents, are heavily invested in the ideology of free markets, which teaches that competitive markets are on the whole self-correcting. These officials and the economists to whom they turn for advice don't like to think of the economy as a kind of epileptic, subject to unpredictable, strange seizures.

And not just *Republican* officials and the economists who advise them. I have elsewhere described President Clinton as the consolidator of the Reagan revolution. His economic policies were shaped by establishment Wall Street figures now in disrepute, such as Robert Rubin, along with economists like Alan Greenspan, a conservative, and Lawrence Summers, a moderate. The many positive experiences with deregulation and privatization, and the many economic success stories that followed the collapse of communism, along with the many failure stories of countries that curtail economic freedom, supported this belief system and made it bipartisan. And it was reinforced, in the case of the financial markets, by the development of the new financial instruments that were believed without good evidence to have increased the resilience of the financial system to shocks.

Bayesian decision theory, systematizing the role of preconceptions in decision-making, teaches that when evidence bearing on a decision is weak, prior beliefs will influence the decision-maker's response to a novel situation—and should, but only to the extent that the preconceptions are grounded in reality. I have said that preconceptions impound knowledge. But the preconceptions that well out of a political ideology are shaped by nonrational factors as well, such as temperament, personal and family history, salient life experiences, religious beliefs, and ethnicity. The play of these factors on businessmen is limited because competition penalizes business decisions based on ideology. Politics and academia are competitive too, but their practitioners are not subject to the harsh discipline of the bottom line.

Second to ideology as a factor that deflected attention from warnings and warning signs was the fact that taking action to reduce the risks warned against would have been costly, quite apart from the fierce opposition it would have aroused in leaders of the business community and their allies in government. Had the Federal Reserve caused interest rates to rise, this would have accelerated the bursting of the housing bubble—and then, since no one could be certain that it *was* a bubble, Congress and the Administration would have been blamed for the fall in home values and the increase in defaults and foreclosures.

As long as the Federal Reserve adjusts interest rates just to maintain price stability and avert or soften recessions—raising interest rates to cool economic activity when inflation threatens and lowering them to stimulate economic activity when recession threatens—its actions are relatively uncontroversial and its political independence is therefore unchallenged. If in addition it tried to prick asset bubbles, as by curtailing bank lending when housing prices soar, it would raise political hackles. Those benefiting from the bubble would deny it was a bubble and sometimes they would be right, and if they were wrong but the bubble was pricked before it had expanded to a very large size there would be great difficulty even after the fact in proving that it had been a bubble. So the Federal Reserve should not be criticized too harshly for having failed to prick the housing bubble in 2005, just as it should not be criticized too harshly for having failed to prick the dot-com stock bubble of the late 1990s, as it could have done by raising the margin requirements for buying stock with borrowed money. It is the passivity of the Federal Reserve between Bear Stearns' collapse in March 2008 and the calamitous collapses in September, and the failure (for which the Fed was jointly responsible with the Treasury Department) to avert Lehman Brothers' bankruptcy, that merit strong criticism.

The point I want to emphasize is that it is very difficult to receive praise, and indeed to avoid criticism, for preventing a bad thing from happening unless the probability of its happening is known. If something unlikely to happen doesn't happen (and, by definition of "unlikely," it usually will not happen), no one is impressed. But people are impressed—unfavorably—by the costs incurred in having prevented the thing that probably wouldn't have happened anyway.

Cassandras are further disliked because it usually is infeasible to take action in response to their warnings. If the prophesied disaster occurs, those who could have taken but did not take preventive action in response to the warnings are blamed for the disaster even if their forbearance was the right decision on the basis of what they knew.

And virtually all warnings are premature, because the date of a warned-against event is likely to be irreducibly uncertain. No one—not even Nouriel Roubini—could predict the day on which the bubble would burst, or indeed the week, month, or year. (Recall the *Economist*'s acknowledgment of having cried wolf in 2002, as it continued to do until at last, four years later, the wolf appeared at the door.) Furthermore, it is impossible to perform a cogent cost-benefit analysis of measures to prevent a contingency from materializing if the probability that it will materialize is unknown. The cost of a disaster has to be discounted (multiplied) by the probability that it will occur, in order to decide how much money should be devoted to reducing that probability. No one could have calculated the probability of a financial crisis such as we are experiencing.

Even if the probability of some adverse event is known and is not trivial, it may not pay to try to prevent it from occurring if the cost of the event if it does occur is unlikely to be very great. It should have been expected that the bursting of the housing bubble would result in a recession centering on the financial markets, because the banks were so heavily invested in risky home loans. But a recession is not a disaster. A depression is, but a depression may have been an unlikely consequence of the housing bubble, the risky lending, and the risky savings. Those conditions spelled recession, for sure, but to turn a recession into the depression that the country is now experiencing may have required additional circumstances, such as the fact that a financial crisis exploded at the climactic phase of a presidential campaign and became acute during the two-and-a-half-month hiatus between the election of the new President and his inauguration. Other fortuities were a lame-duck Congress and a lame-duck President who seemed to lack interest or competence in handling economic issues and to prefer reminiscence, retirement planning, legacy-polishing, and foreign travel to directing, and explaining to the public, the government's response to the biggest economic crisis in three quarters of a century. Still other fortuities were the indecisive, improvised, and inarticulate (though, eventually, aggressive) response to the crisis by government officials; a sudden collapse of much of the automobile industry as a delayed consequence of a surge in gasoline prices exacerbated by the credit crunch (two thirds of all cars are bought on credit); and the deepening of the economic crisis during a Christmas shopping season already foreshortened by a late Thanksgiving (November 27). Desperate to attract Christmas shoppers and avoid an inventory pileup, retailers offered unprecedented discounts. These discounts actually increased after Christmas, some reaching two thirds of the normal price. (The most dramatic of the discounts—two cars for the price of one—was just a 50 percent discount.) By reducing the overall consumer price level, these discounts engendered fears of deflation—the most ominous depression phenomenon.

The probability that *so* many depression-friendly factors would converge just as the economic downturn was accelerating must have been pretty low. But by September the probability of a severe recession was high enough to warrant the government's undertaking costly efforts to try to prevent the risk from materializing. And still the officials dithered. They dithered because they were surprised by the crisis and had no contingency plans for dealing with it. Dithering in response to a financial crisis is especially costly because of the adverse feedback involved in a depression. Once a spiral of falling demand, layoffs, a further fall in demand, more layoffs, and so on begins, it feeds on itself; it requires no external source of nourishment—no further shock to the economy.

Another reason for the failure to anticipate a depression was suggested by a perceptive reader of the Becker-Posner blog, Jamison Davies, who reminded us that important to Roberta Wohlstetter's argument about why the Japanese attack on Pearl

Harbor achieved surprise was that the "signal-to-noise" ratio—the amount of useful information received relative to the amount that is false, misleading, or irrelevant—was low. Distinguishing in a flood of incoming data between those that are genuinely informative and those that are merely noise is exceedingly difficult. Davies points out that "if you give correct warning and act in response to that warning, the attack will likely not materialize (i.e. if the US knew Japan was about to attack Pearl Harbor our defensive preparations would prevent Japan from following through). This means that successful warnings are undercounted because the catastrophe never emerges. This tends to weaken early warning systems as they are perceived to be ineffective even though they may have averted serious problems." Davies adds that "the economic analogy is regulation. Regulations were seen as unnecessary and dismantled because there had been no crises, but policymakers failed to consider that there may have been no crises precisely because of the regulation."

As in the lead-up to the attack on Pearl Harbor, so in the lead-up to the financial crisis that struck in September 2008, most competent analysts disagreed that the economic prospects were as dire as

Roubini and the other "Cassandras," "alarmists," "Eeyores," and "prophets of doom" (notice the absence of a neutral term for someone who warns of disaster—there is no noun "warner") were contending. For all the reasons I have mentioned, most people, even most experts, were unlikely to be persuaded by the doomsters. But it is unforgivable that the government, though alerted by them beginning in 2005 to the signs warning of a possible economic catastrophe, did not deploy its formidable resources to study the issue in depth.

The explanation may be the absence of a machinery (other than the market itself) for aggregating and analyzing information bearing on large-scale economic risk. It is a machinery the Federal Reserve and the Treasury Department could have created, and presumably would have had they not been overconfident that another depression could be prevented more or less effortlessly even after a financial crisis hit, just by a lowering of interest rates.

Little bits of knowledge about the shakiness of the U.S. and global financial systems were widely dispersed among the staffs of banks, other financial institutions, and the regulatory bodies, and among academic economists, financial consultants, accountants, actuaries, rating agencies, mortgage brokers, real estate agents, and business journalists. There was no financial counterpart to the CIA to aggregate and analyze the information—to assemble an intelligible mosaic from the scattered pieces. More precisely, no agency assumed that role, though the Federal Reserve, the Treasury Department, or even the President's Council of Economic Advisers might have done so. Much of the relevant information was proprietary and therefore shielded from journalists and academics. Investment banks, hedge funds, mortgage originators, and other financial firms conceal information about business strategies that might help competitors, and avoid, as far as the law permits (and sometimes farther than it permits), disclosing adverse information about the firm's prospects. Even the regulatory agencies lacked access to much crucial information about the financial system, because of limitations on their authority that were thought appropriate in an era of triumphal deregulation. Lacking authority to regulate the new derivatives, financial regulators could not force disclosure of information that might have revealed how risky the financial system had become. At its peak, the market in credit-default swaps was larger than the entire U.S. stock market (though that is misleading, because swaps are largely offsetting—if an insured event comes to pass, the liability of the issuer and the claim of the purchaser should cancel, as in my A-B example in chapter 2). And because the issuers of the swaps, unlike conventional insurance companies, were not required by law to maintain adequate (or for that matter any) reserves, there was no protection against the kind of run that brought down AIG, leaving the buyers of the swaps uninsured. Home financing was regulated, but by different agencies from those that regulated banks; hedge funds were barely regulated at all.

One might think that if firms are not forthcoming about their strategies, risks, etc., investors will assume the worst, and therefore that competition will force disclosure in much the same way that applicants to law school invariably consent (though permitted by law to withhold their consent) to disclosure of their college grades to the law schools they apply to. But one cannot infer from a firm's caginess about releasing information that it is concealing bad news; it may simply be hiding its insights, strategies, and trade secrets from its competitors.

This analysis helps to explain the puzzling fact

that although the housing bubble began to leak air in 2005, it was not until the fall of 2008 that the government discovered that the banking industry was in dire financial straits. There was bound to be *some* lag between the end of the bubble and the effect on the banks' mortgage-backed securities. A leveling off followed by a fall of housing prices does not affect lenders until the falling prices precipitate defaults, though it will reduce the value of mortgage-backed securities as soon as the market foresees that defaults will reach a level at which the securities, despite being well diversified, will generate less income for their owners than expected and may even imperil principal. Even then bankers will be reluctant to acknowledge that their financial situation has become perilous, lest the acknowledgment cause a run on the bank—the sort of thing that brought down Bear Stearns in March 2008. Even insured depositors may pull their deposits if they think the bank may go under, because they worry about delay in being paid off by the Federal Deposit Insurance Corporation. And not all lenders to banks are fully insured, because until recently there were ceilings on federal deposit insurance; and checkable nonbank accounts, such as an account with a money market fund, were not insured at all. (They are now, and the ceiling on deposit insurance has been taken off.)

Some investors anticipated the effect of the bursting of the housing bubble on mortgage-backed securities and made billions selling short the securities backed by low-rated mortgages. But there was not enough short selling to alert the market and the government to the weakness of the banks, in part because, as noted earlier, short selling is a risky investment strategy. Premature short sellers lose big, and there were many such because of the duration of the housing bubble.

5

The Government Responds

THE GOVERNMENT'S RESPONSE to the crash has moved through four phases, with a fifth that at this writing is wending its way through Congress. The first three phases are collectively the "bailout"; the fourth (running simultaneously with the bailout) I'll call "easy money"; and the fifth will, when executed, be the "stimulus." A small, and as it turned out an ineffectual, stimulus had been tried already; early in 2008 Congress had authorized $168 billion in tax rebates. The amount was too small to have a significant effect in stimulating spending. It was a reminder of the half-measures that Hoover had taken during the Great Depression, before Roosevelt took office.

Still on the drawing board are mortgage relief and comprehensive reform of the regulation of the financial industry. The first I discuss at the end of this chapter, the second briefly in chapter 10; about the second, suffice it here to say that trying to reorganize the financial industry in the midst of a financial crisis risks biting off more than the government will be able to chew.

Bailout (the $700 billion Troubled Asset Relief Program) and easy money began the government's rescue operation. The initial conception of the bailout was that the government would buy the banking industry's "sick" assets—the assets, notably mortgage-backed securities, the value of which had been made uncertain by the collapse of the housing bubble. The premise was that banks were solvent but the market for their sick assets was frozen, and not knowing how thick their equity cushion was the banks were afraid to make loans. The premise proved, as we know, to be mistaken, although it was and is possible that after the banks were given enough capital to restore them to solvency, uncertainty about the value of some of their assets would continue to inhibit them in lending.

In the second bailout iteration, the government invested directly in the biggest banks, bolstering their solvency and in exchange receiving preferred stock—and then complaining under ignorant prodding by Congress that the banks were hoarding their new capital rather than lending it out. But of course—if they were insolvent or potentially so they had to thicken their equity cushion before they could start lending on a large scale, especially since lending is riskier in a depression than in a boom. The banks may also have thought that asset prices would be falling, so best to save money now and invest later (deflation thinking); but this would be difficult to determine. In short, while the government's investing in banks was a sensible measure—the economy needs solvent banks and only the government was willing to contribute the capital needed to assure the banks' solvency—it was unlikely to have large effects in the short run on bank lending.

The form of the investing could be questioned. Preferred stock, despite the name, is debt rather than equity, though as it has no maturity date the corporation doesn't have to worry about its being called. Investing in exchange for preferred stock increased the leverage (though, because of the lack of a maturity date, not the risk) of the banks that received the government's money, making the banks' common stock more volatile than it would otherwise have been, which discouraged private investment. The alternative would have been to contribute equity capital, but that would have made the government an owner or part owner of the banks rather than just a creditor, and there is a natural anxiety about the government's injecting itself that deeply into the central nervous system of a commercial society. Indeed, since the market value of the banks is so depressed, any substantial injection of equity capital would have made the government the majority owner of most of the banks it helped. There is no comparison, so far the magnitude of the government's becoming a major owner of the banking industry is concerned, to the government's takeover in the late 1980s of hundreds of bankrupt savings and loan associations. They were peripheral to the nation's credit system; also they were bankrupt rather than teetering on the brink of bankruptcy, and the government just picked up the pieces.

The government seems about to decide to buy all the "bad" securitized debt owned by banks and put it in a "bad bank." The difference between that and the original buyout plan—the plan that was abandoned in favor of cash transfusions to the bank—is that the "bad bank" (another name for the U.S. Treasury) would buy up *all* the bad securities (and other bad assets, including bad loans) of *all* banks rather than making selective purchases from selected banks. Then the banks' balance sheets would be clean and both management and prospective investors and borrowers would know how safe each bank was. And concerns with favoritism in the allocation of bailout moneys among requesting banks would be allayed.

The government may try to circumvent the problem of valuing the banks' "bad" assets by offering to buy them for their marked-down market value as shown on the banks' books ("marked to market"), and, if they have not been marked down, insuring rather than buying them. There is still a problem—how realistic is an estimate of market value if there is no market?—but it is an improvement over the original plan's unworkable proposal to auction the bad assets. Still, the total cost would be enormous; and neither the valuation problem nor the cost would be avoided by, as has been suggested, the government's "nationalizing"—that is, confiscating—the banks, because it would have to give the owners just compensation. It could let the banks go broke instead and, as in the S&L debacle, pick up the pieces; but that would be no cakewalk either. And many would not go broke, but instead hunker down, hoarding their cash until the economic and regulatory picture cleared.

I will skip ahead for a moment to the fourth phase of the government's response to the depression ("easy money") because it is closely related to the second. In the last week of November 2008 the Federal Reserve announced that it would buy $800 billion of private debt. The purpose, unlike that of the initial bailout, was not to restore liquidity to the banking industry by dispelling uncertainty about the value of the industry's opaque assets; it was to increase the amount of money in circulation in order to revive borrowing and thus avert a decline in personal consumption expenditures and hence in output. But the appetite for borrowing and lending is a function not just of the amount of money in the economy but also of the risk of default, which is high in a depression. That makes it risky to borrow (if you lose your job you may be unable to repay the loan), and makes banks that have their own solvency problems reluctant to lend except at very high interest rates—and the higher the interest rate, the less likely the borrower is to be able to repay the loan.

The third bailout iteration was the federal loan to General Motors and Chrysler in December 2008, made to head off the bankruptcy of these companies or at least defer it. There are, it is essential to understand, two types of corporate bankruptcy—liquidation and reorganization. In a liquidation the bankrupt company closes down, lays off all its workers, and sells all its assets. That would not be the efficient solution to the problems of the Detroit automakers, at least in the near term, even if one ignores (but one shouldn't) the likely effect of such a massive liquidation on the depression. Though deeply uncertain and maybe even despondent about their long-term prospects, the companies can still make and sell millions of motor vehicles annually. They may be losing money on almost every single vehicle that they sell, but at a lower level of production, at which supply and demand would intersect, the price at which they sold their vehicles might exceed the cost of making them.

Suppose an automaker's debt and other fixed costs, divided by the number of cars it sells, is $10,000. The automaker cuts production, lays off workers, closes plants, and slims down to an efficient level of production, given demand and its costs. It will still have a huge burden of debt, the source of my hypothetical $10,000 fixed cost per car. To manufacture a car will not increase the company's fixed costs, and let's assume that it will require materials and labor costing only $20,000. An accountant might say that the cost of making that car was $30,000, and suppose the maximum price that the company can sell the car for is only $25,000. The car still is worth making, because it will enable the company to cover the marginal cost of manufacture, that is, the cost of expanding output by one unit, and will thus reduce the amount of the manufacturer's debt to the tune of $5,000 for every car it makes.

The alternative to liquidation—reorganization—can work well in normal times, as in the bankruptcy of United Air Lines in 2002, provided that the company has good prospects of being able to cover its marginal costs and thus survive if its heavy debt load is reduced or eliminated. In my numerical example the automaker can survive if the debt is cut in half. A company permitted to reorganize in bankruptcy may be able to borrow money to finance its operations no matter how heavy its existing debts are because its post-bankruptcy borrowings ("debtor in possession" loans, as they are called) are given priority over its pre-bankruptcy debts. The old debts will be written down in bankruptcy, reducing the reorganized firm's fixed costs (by $5,000 per car in my example) to a level at which the firm is, it is hoped, once again solvent. The debts that get written down can include health and pension benefits, which in the case of the auto companies continue to be a drag on profitability even though those benefits have been reduced in recent years.

Assuming, therefore, that the companies would be economically viable at a reduced level of production and are broke only because they are crushed by debts contracted when their output was much greater, reorganization in bankruptcy would be the sensible solution to their financial problems. The bankruptcy court could also abrogate the collective bargaining contracts between the automakers and the United Auto Workers. That would allow the automakers to slash wages and benefits— and a drastic reduction in labor costs may well be essential to their long-term survival.

But this rosy picture belongs to normal times. There were three problems with allowing the automakers to be forced into bankruptcy just as the nation was sliding into a depression. The first was that the companies might have had to liquidate, even though they have going-concern value provided that their production is cut and their debts and their labor costs reduced. They might have had to liquidate because of inability to attract the substantial debtor-in-possession loans that they would have needed to enable them to survive while undergoing reorganization. The distress of the banking industry made it unlikely that banks would make the huge risky loans necessary to keep the auto companies afloat.

Second, not only the size of the Detroit auto-makers but also peculiarities of the industry would have made bankruptcy likely to exacerbate the nation's miserable economic condition. If, having declared bankruptcy, the automakers were unable to attract the necessary debtor-in-possession loans and therefore could not reorganize and instead had to liquidate, not only would more than 200,000 autoworkers find themselves unemployed but so would hundreds of thousands of employees of automobile-parts suppliers and automobile dealers. All told, some 3 million workers are employed directly or indirectly by General Motors, Ford, and Chrysler. And if the firms were able to reorganize in bankruptcy rather than having to liquidate, and thus continued producing, the decline in their sales probably would accelerate. Many consumers would be scared off by the uncertainties associated with bankruptcy, especially the bankruptcy of an auto manufacturer. They would worry: Will warranties be honored? Will parts be available? Will the dealership from which one bought a car survive? Will service standards slip? What about the car's resale value? Consumers would disbelieve any soothing assurances by government officials that bankruptcy is no big deal for the customers of the bankrupt firm as long as it does not liquidate; all the other soothing assurances by the government about the financial crisis have proved unfounded; and reorganization might fail because of the crisis. Because motor vehicles are highly durable, it is easy to be prudent and defer replacing one's existing vehicle until the future of the manufacturers becomes clear.

Granted, with General Motors and Chrysler having announced that they had hired bankruptcy lawyers and were suspending much of their North American production for months, the public is becoming aware that the Detroit automobile industry is bankrupt in all but name. But the psychological impact of a formal bankruptcy of much of the U.S. auto industry (not all, since the part of the industry owned by foreign companies is solvent) in the midst of a depression could still be great. The impact would not be just psychological. Existing warranties would be unsecured debts in bankruptcy, and probably worth very little. Owners would realize that unless their warranty had already expired, their car would now be worth less and they would be facing higher maintenance expenses than they had reckoned with. If they realized that existing warranties would be worth little or nothing in bankruptcy but that warranties issued by a bankrupt automaker would be fully enforceable (as post-bankruptcy-petition debt, like the debt created by debtor-in-possession loans), they would wait to buy a Detroit car until the manufacturer declared bankruptcy.

Already, as we know, consumers—rendered fearful by repeated misinformation from government officials concerning the gravity of the economic situation (officials would not acknowledge that the nation was even in a recession until long after it was obvious to the man in the street that we were in something worse)—are reducing their buying. This is precipitating big layoffs in the retail sector, which in turn reduce buying power, which in turn spurs more layoffs. This vicious cycle would be accelerated by the laying off of an immense number of workers if efforts at reorganization in bankruptcy failed and the automakers liquidated. The firms should be kept out of the bankruptcy court until the depression bottoms out and the economy begins to grow again. The government's bailout of the airlines after the drastic decline in flying that followed the 9/11 attacks (airlines are constantly teetering on the edge of bankruptcy because of their very high fixed costs—costs that by definition do not fall when output falls) allowed United Air Lines to have an orderly bankruptcy reorganization beginning the following year and ending in 2006.

The federal loan to the automakers was an executive-branch initiative taken in the waning days of the Bush Administration after Congress failed to pass an auto-bailout bill. The combination (no bill, but approximately the same relief) was politically ingenious—it produced a victory for both political parties, underscoring the fact that a depression is a political as well as an economic event. The Republican senators stood up for their principles— that freedom to fail is basic to capitalism, that wages and benefits should be set by competition in free labor markets rather than by powerful unions (which are worker cartels), that government should not manage businesses, and that government expenditures should be minimized. The Republican senators were also standing up for the interests of Toyota and the other foreign manufacturers that have plants in the United States; for those plants are mainly in the South, the stronghold of the Republican Party. In addition, by opposing an auto bailout Republican senators distanced themselves from the Bush Administration, which was both unpopular and believed by many Republicans to have betrayed Republican small-government principles. And though a collapse of the domestic auto industry that would have deepened the depression would have exposed the Republican senators to criticism, they knew that the executive branch would bail out the auto industry without new legislation.

The Republican Party looked crushed after the November election. But congressional Republicans quickly rallied, became notably assertive, have scored some victories, and may complicate and delay the Obama Administration's programs for fighting the depression.

Secretary of the Treasury Paulson had taken the position that he lacked authority under existing law to bail out the automakers. But as soon as Congress voted down the bailout bill he changed his mind, thus reinforcing the impression that our top financial officials are floundering, and further undermining his and Bernanke's claim to have lacked legal authority to bail out Lehman Brothers, whose collapse was one of the principal triggering events of the depression. If executive officials could bail out bankrupt auto manufacturers, they could have bailed out a bankrupt investment bank.

In supporting the auto bailout bill the Democrats scored points with their constituencies by standing up for union workers, for the "greening" of the automobile industry, for states in which the domestic auto industry is centered that voted Democratic in the recent election (Michigan, Ohio, and Indiana), for the principle of active government, and for trying to avert a deepening of the current depression.

The auto-bailout bill had earned the ire of Republican senators because of its failure to lean hard on the collective bargaining agreements negotiated by the United Auto Workers, because of the divided control of the industry that the bill created—divided among the manufacturers, a federal "car czar," and intrusive congressional oversight— and because of the considerable element of fantasy in the idea that Congress plus the President can revitalize the domestic auto industry. Nowhere is it written that the United States, let alone the states in which the domestic auto manufacturers are centered, has a comparative advantage over other countries, or other regions of the United States, in manufacturing motor vehicles. Evidently it does not, and Congress and the President cannot change that, as Japan learned from the failure of the "industrial policy" administered by its once-admired Ministry of International Trade and Industry.

The realistic goal of an auto bailout is not to reform, revitalize, or restructure the industry. It is to postpone bankruptcy until the end of the depression is in sight and consumer confidence restored to the point at which such a bankruptcy can be taken in stride. To attain this goal did not require imposing conditions on the use that the auto manufacturers made of the bailout money. Those conditions, which appeared in watered-down form in the executive-branch substitute for the failed bailout bill, were not an economic but a political necessity, because of widespread anger at the incompetence of the industry—a majority of Americans oppose *any* bailout of automakers. The conditions are a mistake from a purely economic standpoint. They require merely *negotiation* over measures for restoring the industry to solvency, and thus set the stage for a game of chicken that, like the games of chicken played by teenage drivers, can result in a wreck. The union, for example, may refuse to make substantial concessions and instead challenge the government to allow the automakers to go broke, hoping that the threat either will cause the companies' managers and bondholders to make the concessions necessary to avert bankruptcy or induce further bailouts by the government.

At the very least, the Obama Administration had to be allowed to decide the fate of the auto companies. That was the compelling reason for the $17 billion in loans that the Bush Administration agreed to give them to keep them breathing until the end of the first quarter of 2009. But it gave the union an incentive to drag its heels until the arrival of the presumptively more friendly President and Congress.

The fifth phase of the response to the depression is the planned "stimulus." As proposed by Democratic congressmen and now passed by the House of Representatives and awaiting Senate action, the American Recovery and Reinvestment Act of 2009 would authorize the federal government to spend $819 billion over two years beyond what the government would otherwise be spending during that period. A third of the proposed budget-busting stimulus package is earmarked for tax reductions and the rest is split between public-works programs, such as road construction and measures to reduce carbon emissions, and transfer payments that would increase unemployment benefits, food-stamp entitlements, federal subsidies for health care, and other social-welfare expenditures and that would make up for some of the sharp decline (due to the depression) in the states' tax revenues and ability to borrow.

The logic of such a response is straightforward. Private consumption has fallen and is expected to continue to fall because a very large number of people have found themselves worse off than they expected to be and, lacking adequate savings, have decided to consume significantly less than they had been doing in the recent past. The result of their decisions has been to idle productive resources that were needed to sustain the higher level of consumption that preceded the depression. With potential supply exceeding actual demand, government hopes that it can restore balance—raise $X - Y$ to X, in my earlier formulation—by using its fiscal powers to augment demand and, by doing so, to stimulate producers to restore output to where it was before the depression.

Most conservatives prefer the tax cut to the other

elements of the stimulus program because it does not redistribute wealth and it keeps government from meddling with markets. Most liberals prefer public spending because it expands the role of government and can be targeted on improving the welfare of the worst-off people in society. The worst-off are disproportionately unemployed, but tax cuts benefit mainly the well-off—they are the people who pay most of the taxes. And while it is true that recipients of unemployment benefits are required to pay income tax on those benefits, many of the unemployed have a total income, including benefits, that is below the cutoff point for taxable income.

One problem with tax cuts as a response to the depression is that many people will save rather than spend the increase in their after-tax income in order to rebuild their now meager savings and stave off insolvency, especially if they don't think the tax cut will be permanent. Only 15 percent of the $168 billion in tax rebates that Congress decreed in the spring of 2008 was spent. Even in normal times, people spend less out of temporary income spurts than they do when they receive what they think will be a permanent increase in their income, because they would not be able to maintain the higher standard of living that the spurt would temporarily enable. Keynes made a related point (*The General Theory*, p. 97): in short periods "habits . . . are not given time enough to adapt themselves to changed objective circumstances. For a man's habitual standard of life usually has the first claim on his income, and he is apt to save the difference which discovers itself between his actual income and the expense of his habitual standard." (The difference between the permanent-income hypothesis and the habit hypotheses is that the first implies that behavior will change immediately upon a permanent change in income while the second implies a lag because of the drag that habit exerts on changing one's behavior.) Economists who favor tax cuts over deficit spending argue, therefore, that any tax cut should be permanent. But there is no such thing as a permanent tax cut, because the Congress that enacts a tax cut cannot bind subsequent Congresses (there is a new one every two years) not to rescind it. Moreover, basic to a sensible program of emergency anti-depression deficit spending is that the spending should indeed be temporary, and end when the depression ends.

Otherwise the government can find itself facing horrendous budget deficits for the indefinite future.

The tax rebates that Congress approved in February 2008 were a damp squib so far as stimulating increased consumption was concerned. The tax cut in the stimulus package is only two-thirds greater. The difference in size is too small to make a big difference, or perhaps any difference. Taxpayers may save an even higher percentage of this tax cut than of the rebate because there is greater economic anxiety now.

The part of the tax cut that is saved will increase the amount of capital available for lending unless the savings take ultra-safe forms—but they may. And individuals do not lend to business; they lend to banks or other financial intermediaries that do the actual lending, and the intermediaries may decide to invest additional money they receive from individuals in government securities in order to reduce the amount of leverage, and therefore risk, in their capital structure. Moreover, any effect of a tax cut or rebate in increasing lending to the private sector may be offset by the government's increased borrowing to finance the tax cut.

A federal tax cut will do nothing to alleviate the acute financial problems of the states. They have seen their tax revenues drop sharply, yet they cannot create money, or engage in deficit spending without borrowing at high interest rates. If federal tax rates were reduced, states could raise their tax rates without increasing the net tax burden of their citizens. But that would be a time-consuming adjustment even if the political opposition to raising taxes during a depression could be overcome. It would be ironic if instead of federal money being spent on improving infrastructure, federal taxes were cut, state taxes raised, and the new state tax moneys used to finance many of the infrastructure projects that federal moneys would otherwise finance. All that would have been gained would have been delay in responding to the economic crisis — quite serious delay with respect to those state projects, interrupted because of state fiscal problems, that could resume on short notice if federal moneys were available but must otherwise wait for state legislatures to vote higher taxes.

The transfer-payments component of the proposed stimulus is also questionable, though politically irresistible. The goal of a deficit-spending program aimed at combating a depression is to restore demand to its pre-depression level, not to expand it beyond that level. If instead of demand rising as a consequence of the program from $X - Y$ to X (the pre-depression level), it rises from $X - Y$ to $X + Z$, there will be inflation because demand will exceed supply. Programs to transfer wealth are very difficult to abolish because interest groups form about them. That is why there is a danger of excess demand after the depression ends. But perhaps we can't afford to look ahead that far. The transfer-payments component of the stimulus package is superior to tax cuts because it puts money in the hands of more people who are too poor to save much and who will therefore spend the money and by doing so increase the demand for goods and services, which is the aim of deficit spending in a depression. Yet even so straightforward a transfer program as extending unemployment benefits is problematic, as it will make unemployed people pickier about jobs and thus delay their reemployment.

I note parenthetically that the transfer proposals illustrate the inadequacy of "automatic stabilizers" as a depression antidote. In a recession, people pay less income tax because their income is lower, and unemployment benefits replace (not fully of course) wages, and both effects moderate the impact of a recession on spending without need for any new legislative or other policies. The automatic stabilizers, which existed in only a rudimentary form at the outset of the Great Depression, were among the policy innovations that made most macroeconomists confident that there would never be another depression.

The danger that a spending program adopted in order to promote recovery from a depression will become a permanent drain on the federal budget is less serious with respect to public-works programs (the third component of the stimulus package), especially road-building and other infrastructure projects, and especially those infrastructure projects that were planned or begun by states or municipalities and deferred because of the fall in the states' tax revenues (and their ability to borrow) caused by the depression. The federal government can finance these projects until the depression is over; the states can then continue them, if they want, with their own tax money.

From the standpoint of being able to end an expensive antidepression program when the depression ends, a public-works program is best and a nontax transfer program worst. Taxes are raised and lowered pretty frequently, but a transfer program, being targeted to a particular, often narrow, group, creates expectations and a sense of entitlement that make termination politically very difficult.

Reducing unemployment through deficit spending on public works has additional advantages. The dramatic drop in income and, what may be even more important, in confidence about future employment prospects that unemployment creates is likely to trigger a steeper fall in consumption than the lesser drop in income, and lesser anxiety about the future, experienced in a depression by people who still have jobs. And the higher the unemployment rate, the more the still-employed will worry about losing their jobs. That worry will give them an incentive to reduce consumption that a tax cut is unlikely to offset; they will save the tax cut as insurance against future unemployment. These are reasons to think that deficit-spending programs that reduce unemployment are more effective in fighting a depression than tax cuts or other transfers.

Deficit spending on public works has a multiplier effect on output, which the other forms of deficit spending do not. When the government finances road construction, it not only creates additional demand for labor and materials and so stimulates output; it puts more money in the hands of the construction workers and the suppliers of building materials, and both groups will spend part of that money on buying goods and services themselves, further stimulating output. It has been estimated that every dollar spent on public works in a recession or depression increases spending by $1.40, though this is one of the roughest of rough estimates and some economists think the multiplier is less than $1.

Deficit spending on public works requires borrowing and thus leads to higher interest rates, which can choke off a recovery from a depression. But tax cuts and other transfer payments have the same effect because they increase the federal deficit too and thus the amount of money that the government must borrow. All forms of deficit spending, by the way, could in principle be paid for by the Federal Reserve rather than by the government's borrowing the money. The Federal Reserve can increase the supply of money and use some of its newly created money to pay government contractors. But we shall see later in this chapter that there are practical limitations on how much the Fed can expand the money supply to fight the depression.

A big problem with the public-works approach is the inevitable delays in beginning to spend project funds. That is an advantage of the transfer-payment part of the stimulus package and is also why the public-works approach has been found to be ineffectual in dealing with mild recessions—they are over before a program of public works is implemented in time to have a significant effect on employment and output. Unless the government just hires all the unemployed to rake leaves in their backyards, public-works projects will require substantial lead time. Months will be consumed in identifying and designing each project and laying in necessary materials and signing necessary contracts before a project actually gets under way. But the problem of delay may be mitigable, as I have already hinted, by concentrating resources on projects that have been interrupted by the economic downturn and can be resumed on short notice. A number of projects started or scheduled to start by states and municipalities fall into this category. Moreover, business forecasters expect the current downturn not only to worsen but also to be more protracted than the usual recession (the expected protraction is one of the reasons to think we're in a depression). The more protracted it is, the more time a public-works program will have to increase employment and output.

The problem of delay is not unique to the public-works response to a depression. Do not think that when the Federal Reserve increases banks' lending capacity there is an immediate uptick in economic activity. The bank has to decide what kind of loans to make and to whom. (People who receive a tax cut or other benefits likewise have to decide what to spend their additional money on.) Maybe the bank will decide to lend the money abroad—or to the federal government, by buying Treasury bonds—or use it to buy another bank, or wait to buy bonds or other assets when they are cheaper. Maybe it will have trouble lending the money because people are afraid to take on more debt even at what normally would be attractive interest rates. And maybe they won't be attractive rates, because the banks are fearful of defaults. If people do borrow, it will take time for them to spend the money, and they may not spend it in ways that increase output.

A further problem is identifying worthwhile public projects—projects that would create real value—and, having identified them, choosing to fund them rather than projects favored by politicians on political instead of economic grounds. Not that there is a dearth of public projects that would confer social benefits; there are even projects that might yield net benefits greater than those of equivalent private spending. Possible candidates are investments in transportation infrastructure, control of climate change, preservation of biodiversity, prison construction, education at all levels, scientific research, children's health, other public health—such as control of obesity and preventive measures against pandemics, including pandemics that might be started by terrorists—and increasing the size of the army and replacing equipment lost in the Iraq and Afghanistan wars.

A number of the investments proposed in the Recovery and Reinvestment Act are at least plausible candidates to be social-welfare-enhancing. But one of the best candidates is slated to receive a meager $5 billion—investing in the military. Losses of equipment in the wars in Iraq and Afghanistan have been made up out of inventory as well as by new production, and as a result inventories have been allowed to run down and have to be built up again. This can be done swiftly, and almost all the equipment of our armed forces is produced in the United States, so there should be a direct as well as an immediate effect on unemployment. The Obama Administration has responded that the military did not request more of the stimulus package. But of course not; the military doesn't want its priorities determined by civilian needs.

Given politics, it is a fair guess (it is actually a certainty) that many of the projects in the stimulus program will yield costs in excess of their benefits—at least if one ignores the benefits that such projects confer on fighting the depression, as distinct from simply improving the nation's transportation system, education system, etc. That is a vital qualification, and though obvious is overlooked by many opponents of the stimulus package. In evaluating a project designed to fight a depression, one must not ignore the benefits of fighting it successfully! Even spending on worthless projects can be an effective and, paradoxically, a rather cheap response to a depression.

Suppose there is a great deal of unemployment in the construction industry—and there is, because of the bursting of the housing bubble and the ensuing decline in the amount of home building and now of other construction as well. The government decides to build a chain of luxurious no-kill shelters for feral cats in areas of the country in which the unemployment rate of construction workers is particularly high. A cost-benefit analysis reveals that the cost of the program will be $10 million and the benefit—were there no depression—only $1 million (what the cat lovers would have been willing to pay for the shelters). But if the workers who would be employed to build the shelters and the suppliers of the building materials would otherwise remain unemployed, the project will increase demand. The workers and suppliers will have higher incomes and greater confidence about the economic future and thus will spend more on goods and services and also cost the government less in unemployment and welfare benefits and pay more in taxes. Moreover, if the workers and suppliers really have no alternative employment opportunities, the cost of the shelters will be small. A resource is costly only if it has valuable alternative use ("opportunity cost"). If the alternative to building a cat shelter is collecting unemployment benefits, the cost to society of the construction worker's time building the shelter is limited to the value to him of leisure, that is, of not working. That cost is likely to be small relative to the benefits if the project reduces the severity of the depression.

What is informative about this ridiculous example is that after the depression was over there would be little pressure for further appropriations for building cat shelters. The greatest danger of an ambitious program of public spending is the momentum that it creates to continue it after the depression is over, because interest groups will form around the program. Conservatives worry rightly that a depression can provide the occasion for an enduring expansion of government based on the pretext of a temporary need for increased government spending; they see in the health-benefits provisions of the Recovery and Reinvestment Act the opening wedge for national health insurance. And while it is always possible to include a "sunset" clause in legislation, there is no way to prevent a subsequent Congress from deleting the clause. And the clause would be an acknowledgment that the program might have no long-run benefits but was strictly an emergency response—an acknowledgment that believers in the long-term benefits of the program would be reluctant to make. Remember too that temporary income is more likely to be saved than spent; a sunset clause would signal that the increased income from the program might indeed prove temporary.

Lack of momentum is one reason that the least

questionable component of the stimulus is spending on transportation (or other construction-intensive) infrastructure. One might wish therefore that it were a larger component; some senators, to their credit, are pushing for such an expansion. The bill passed by the House of Representatives allots only $90 billion of the $819 billion stimulus to transportation infrastructure—$30 billion for highway construction, $31 billion for energy savings in federal and other public facilities, $19 billion for flood control and environmental improvements, and $10 billion for transit and rail.

But the $90 billion figure is a little misleading, because other parts of the act allot money to other construction projects, such as constructing or repairing school buildings and hospitals, and the real unit of analysis should be construction rather than infrastructure; there is a construction industry but not an infrastructure industry. An advantage of investing in transportation infrastructure, however, is that the cost of improvements can be recouped by tolls or other user taxes after the depression ends, whereas the construction or renovation of public schools, for example, could not be financed by user taxes but would require a general tax increase. Another advantage of investing in transportation infrastructure is that much of the investment can take (and is planned to take) the form of repairing existing infrastructure rather than of creating new infrastructure, and the lead time for repair projects is short.

I am assuming that the construction projects that the act will finance will create real value, unlike the "bridge to nowhere" proposed for Alaska. Otherwise the user fees will really just be taxes. But as long as the money allocated to construction is for projects that have been authorized but have been interrupted or deferred, or merely accelerates projects scheduled to begin on a later date (accelerates them in order to increase output and employment now), there will be no waste beyond what was built into the original plan for the project.

The point about acceleration is important from the standpoint of cost minimization. Suppose that were it not for the depression, certain bridges and highways that are reaching the end of their normal lifespan would not be rebuilt for another five years, but because we are in a depression there are unemployed labor and material resources that could be productively employed to do the rebuilding this year or next at a cost savings that would exceed the benefits from delaying the projects for five years.

Accelerating the rebuilding would then be an efficient anti-depression measure.

There is always a danger that a public-works program will "crowd out" private investment by bidding scarce resources away from the private sector; imagine the government's borrowing money from a bank that would otherwise lend the money to a private contractor. But the danger of crowding out is reduced, for construction projects at any rate, by the very large number of unemployed construction workers—more than 100,000 were added to the unemployment rolls in December 2008 alone. They are unemployed because there is no private demand for their labor. In time they can find jobs in other industries, but in the interim, if they are unemployed, the economic crisis will worsen.

In general, moreover, crowding out is less of a worry in a depression that involves widespread banking failures and a resulting impairment of financial intermediation and a decline in private borrowing. Maybe there are great private projects on the drawing board, but if the projectors cannot attract investment, the projects will stay there. The government does not have to go through financial intermediaries to finance a project. And if people want to save more but are afraid of risky savings, so that savings available for investment in productive activities shrink, the government's borrowing to invest in such activities will not displace private investment.

Still another advantage of deficit spending on construction is that the inputs used in construction are mainly of domestic rather than of foreign origin—not only labor but also most of the materials. This is important because the purchase of foreign inputs increases employment abroad rather than at home. Picking projects that use mainly U.S. inputs is better than attaching "Buy American" conditions to the projects authorized by the stimulus bill. The last thing we need is a trade war. What is more, projects conditioned on buying American inputs are bound to be inefficient, as the need to attach such a condition implies that a product is produced more efficiently abroad.

One thing that must give pause is the problem of substitutability across construction projects. Building a house and building a highway are not interchangeable activities. Unemployment in the construction industry may be concentrated in residential construction, and residential-construction workers may not have the right skills for highway or bridge construction, let alone for flood control.

(What use is a plumber or a carpenter in building a highway?) The more specialized the American workforce has become, the less effect public-works projects are likely to have on employment. And if the projects do not reduce unemployment but instead compete with private employers for workers, the only effect may be to increase the national debt and create a future inflation.

This is a general concern rather than anything peculiar to construction. In fact it is a greater concern with some of the other projects proposed in the American Recovery and Reinvestment Act. Projects designed to promote efficient use of energy (in order to limit global warming and dependence on foreign oil—worthy objectives, however) will create inflationary pressure by bidding for scarce resources against the private sector, such as scientific and engineering skills and complex, novel technologies. That is a compelling reason for concentrating the stimulus in the industries in which unemployment is greatest.

A further cautionary note is sounded by what is widely believed (though has not been proved) to be the failure of deficit spending in the parallel situation that Japan faced in the 1990s. A bank-financed housing bubble had burst and banks took it on the chin. The government's main response was massive deficit spending on public works, but if indeed it was ineffective, this may have been because the banks were not given enough new capital, so that credit remained scarce and private demand was slow to revive. The bailouts and "easy money" responses to our depression address that problem, though how effectively may be doubted—if banks are hesitant to lend, giving them more capital may not overcome their hesitation, especially in a deflation. But at least Americans don't have the same propensity to save as the Japanese, and "excessive" saving can feed deflation, as we are about to see.

Even if deficit spending will work better for us than it did for the Japanese, the increased federal deficit caused by an ambitious public-works program not financed out of taxes—at the same time that tax collections are declining because taxpayers' incomes are declining—may give rise to inflation after the depression ends. Or may not: if deficit spending increases output, the ratio of money to output need not increase. That the ratio remains constant is actually very important to a recovery from the depression. If the money supply did not expand with output, there would be deflation, which is more dangerous to an economy than inflation.

Still, at the end of its deficit-spending spree, the government will have greater debt. It can pay off the debt in cheaper dollars (inflation), or it can raise taxes and allocate the additional tax revenue to paying off the debt. Whether it can go the tax route will depend, however, on how much borrowing it will have done to combat the depression and therefore how high taxes will have to be raised in order to pay off the debt. We must avoid creating a future tax burden so heavy that it will seriously distort the allocation of resources—not to mention choke off recovery from the depression.

What would be sure to create inflation would be a deficit-spending program that did more than replace the shortfall in the private demand for goods and services with additional public demand. Suppose private demand falls by 10 percent; if the government increases its demand for goods and services to a level at which combined private and public demand is higher than before the depression, when the nation's economic resources were more or less fully employed, then more money will be chasing fewer goods and services, and there will

be inflation. Some economists worry that the unemployment rate is not high enough to create any
room for increased public demand that will not
create inflation. But the unemployment rate is increasing, and anyway the stimulus package, despite
its apparent size, is modest relative to the size of
the economy; $819 billion spread over two years is
only about 3 percent of gross domestic product,
and the unemployment rate may hit 10 percent by
the end of 2009. The longer a recession or depression lasts, the more unemployment there will be,
because in every period a new cohort of young people graduate from (or quit) school and try to enter
the workforce, while many older workers will delay
their retirement because of the negative effect of
the depression on their wealth. And unemployment figures underestimate the degree to which
labor is being underutilized, since they exclude
part-time workers who would like to work full-time,
able-bodied workers who have given up looking for
work or decided to get some more education instead, and workers nudged into retiring who are too
old to have a realistic prospect of landing another
full-time job.

Another danger is that when the stimulus ends,
demand will fall and we will be back to where we

were before the stimulus; it will be like a driver's taking his foot off the accelerator. But that is unlikely if the stimulus succeeds in expanding output. It is true that when the infrastructure projects end, many of the construction workers employed on them will be unemployed, for one effect of the housing bubble was to increase the number of construction workers and it will be a while before we have another housing bubble (one hopes). But it will be easier for the laid-off construction workers to find jobs in other industries when the depression ends because the overall unemployment rate will be lower. The stimulus imparted by our military expenditures in World War II ended when the war ended, but the country did not return to its pre-war economic condition. Military production facilities were converted to civilian production and the returning soldiers were effortlessly reintegrated into the new, postwar—post-stimulus—economy.

From the foregoing discussion, we can distill criteria for an optimal depression-fighting stimulus program. It should be targeted on industries or areas of the country where there is high unemployment or other unemployed resources. It should be executable on short notice, without long delays for planning, contracting, and so forth. It should be terminable when the depression ends. And it should have net social value (as a feral-cat shelter program would not) apart from its contribution to ending the depression. Does the proposed stimulus package meet these criteria? Of course not. Is it therefore an $800 billion mistake, as the economist Martin Feldstein has called it?

To answer the question requires recognizing the political dimension of the depression. By arousing memories of the extraordinary legislative accomplishments at the very outset of Franklin Roosevelt's Administration, the depression has created an opportunity for President Obama to achieve much of his legislative agenda at the very outset of his Administration, when his political power is at its zenith. But to seize the opportunity he must present his legislative package as a response to the depression, and therefore as a stimulus. Parts or even all of it may have some effect in stimulating output and employment, though less than if it were designed solely to ameliorate the economic situation. Economists miss its dual purpose and criticize it for not being a laser-beam attack on the depression. In doing so, they miss the point.

The combined expense of the bailouts provided or authorized to date and the projected $819 billion stimulus package, which at this writing seems likely to grow to at least $900 billion, is $2 trillion, and seems certain to grow. Some and perhaps a great deal of the bailout money will be recovered by the eventual sale of the preferred stock that the government is acquiring in exchange for helping the banks to recapitalize, and by the repayment of some or all of the loans that the government has made as part of the bailout, for example the loans to General Motors and Chrysler. Because part or even all of the bailout debt may eventually be re-paid, the stimulus will be costlier dollar for dollar of federal outlays than the bailouts, although some of its cost will be recouped in higher tax revenues if the spending succeeds in stimulating economic ac-tivity. And the recoupment of bailout money could be offset by defaults on the $2.3 trillion of debt that the government has newly guaranteed; this num-ber too will grow.

The national debt on the eve of the bailouts was $10 trillion—almost double what it had been in 2000, the increase being due to the huge budget deficits run by the Bush Administration. To this must be added at least some of the trillions of dol-lars in anti-depression programs, plus an increase in the chronic federal budget deficit because of falling tax revenues due to the depression. It would not be surprising if the national debt reached $12 trillion by the end of this year. That would be a 20 percent increase and would increase the national debt from 70 percent of current gross domestic product (which is about $14 trillion a year) to 84 percent.

In 2007 the United States ranked twenty-seventh among nations in the ratio of national debt to GDP. An increase to 84 percent would boost us to twelfth, equivalent to Belgium, and among other developed countries we would be below only Japan (170 percent), Italy (104 percent), Singapore (96 percent), and Greece (90 percent) and just ahead of Norway (83 percent). Comparisons are misleading because national debt will be soaring in almost all nations as they combat what is truly a global depression. But all that demand for loans to finance national debt will increase the interest rate that the United States will have to pay in order to finance the additional national debt that we are taking on, as well as to replace existing debt as it comes due. That is a worrisome prospect. Higher interest rates will both retard recovery from the depression and make it more difficult to finance government services without imposing taxes so high as to further retard the recovery and reduce economic efficiency generally. We must not be deceived by the fact that at present interest rates on Treasury securities are low. In a global depression, those securities are a safe haven. When the U.S. and world economies recover, the demand for Treasury securities will fall and the cost to the government of borrowing will therefore rise.

If the public debt of the United States were financed by Americans, the higher interest rates neccssary to pay it down when it became as huge as it has become would transfer wealth from one group of Americans to another; it would not impoverish the country. But the public debt is increasingly owned by foreigners, and repaying them will reduce Americans' wealth.

The bank-bailout/easy-money responses to the depression (they are similar in their focus on increasing credit) and the stimulus response (deficit spending) reflect the two principal competing theories of how the recession triggered by the 1929 stock market crash could have been prevented from becoming a severe depression. One, the monetarist theory, is that the Federal Reserve should not have let the money supply fall so low as to engender deflation. (A variant is that we should have gone off the gold standard before 1933, because adherence to the gold standard limited the Federal Reserve's ability to expand the money supply.) The other, the Keynesian theory, is that the government should have engaged in large-scale deficit spending on public works in order to reduce unemployment and by so doing stimulate output and (eventually) private spending. The public-works approach was followed in the 1930s by Hitler's Germany and imperial Japan with considerable success, albeit success full of future menace. The tax cuts and benefits enhancements proposed in the Recovery and Reinvestment Act are variants rather than components of that approach.

The two basic remedial approaches correspond to two theories of the cause of the Great Depression: the monetarist—that it was caused by the Federal Reserve's allowing the money supply to shrink, causing deflation—and the Keynesian—that private demand for goods and services fell drastically in the wake of the stock market crash and the bank insolvencies triggered by it and that the ensuing diminution in the money supply resulted from, rather than caused, the reduction in economic activity; there was less demand for money. A third causal theory, though similar to the second, is that the depression was the product of a credit binge in the 1920s, in part due to the creation of new forms of consumer credit, such as installment purchasing, as well as the purchase of stocks with money borrowed from banks.

Economists are divided not only about the causes of the 1930s depression but also on how best to treat a depression (as distinct from a mere recession)—whether with bailouts designed to recapitalize the banking system; easy money; or deficit spending in the form of public investment (public-works programs), tax cuts, or transfer payments. The easy-money approach comes in two flavors. The first is the purchase by the Federal Reserve of government securities owned by commercial banks, to increase the money supply and thus reduce interest rates and stimulate borrowing and lending. The second is the purchase by the Fed of other debts, to improve the issuers' balance sheets and thus encourage lending. So there are six different measures for fighting a depression (with countless variants), and the government is doing or planning to do all six. (Eight, if we include reregulation of banking and mortgage relief, though the latter is a bailout measure in a broad sense—a bailout of mortgagors rather than of banks and auto companies.)

I have discussed the limitations of the fiscal solutions; to understand the limitations of the monetarist solution we need to consider how the Federal Reserve creates money. We should not think of it as a matter of running the printing presses in the Bureau of Engraving and Printing faster and scattering the additional dollar bills produced by the speed-up as if they were confetti. Instead the Federal Reserve buys short-term federal securities from banks, crediting each bank's account in a federal reserve bank with the amount of the purchase. The transaction gives the bank greater reserves, which allow it to lend more—much more, since a bank is allowed to lend a multiple of its reserves.

So really all that's involved (putting to one side the mechanics, which include reducing the federal funds rate, which is the price of bank reserves, and reducing banks' reserve requirements directly, as well as the purchase of federal securities that I have just described) is that the Federal Reserve, when it wants to expand the money supply, lets banks write bigger checks. When loan money is deposited in a borrower's bank account, the amount of money in the economy is increased. So the more loans a bank is permitted to and does make, the more the bank accounts of people and firms swell. Since interest is the cost of money, the more money there is sloshing around in the economy, the lower interest rates are likely to be, though there is no certainty of this because interest rates, especially long-term interest rates, are influenced by other factors besides the supply of money, such as the risk of default and expectations of higher inflation. Even when interest rates are very low, there may be little demand for loans if people are already overindebted. Since, moreover, the Federal Reserve's efforts to expand or contract the money supply and so lower or raise interest rates are mediated by the banks, a breakdown in the banking system can loosen the Federal Reserve's control over the money supply, opening the way to deflation. That is why the kind of shock to the economy that comes from a banking crisis is potentially more serious than a shock created by a technological change.

Increasing the money supply reduces the value of money, and so creates a threat of inflation, because, initially at least, more money is buying the same amount of goods and services. But in a depression the threat of inflation lies in the future. The immediate danger is the opposite. If a bank's equity cushion is too thin for comfort, the bank is unlikely to thin it further by converting its safest assets into risky loans—as an increased fraction of loans are bound to be during a depression—even if invited and enabled to do so by the Federal Reserve's increasing the bank's reserves. If banks are frightened to lend, then instead of using their capital to make loans they will use it to buy utterly safe securities, such as short-term Treasury bills. The increased demand for these securities will drive the interest rate on them down—in fact *has* driven it down, virtually to zero. In this situation, if the government buys Treasury bills from the banks, the banks will just be exchanging one kind of safe security—a Treasury bill—for another—cash, which they might use just to buy more Treasury bills!

If, fearing for their solvency, banks do not increase their lending when the government increases their reserves—and if individuals, fearing for their solvency, do not want to borrow—the danger of deflation looms. And it is deflation that made the Great Depression "great."

Without bank lending, personal consumption expenditures fall sharply (for remember that borrowing and lending are the means by which present consumption is maintained at a high level), causing the price level to fall as sellers try desperately to retain their customers. We've seen intimations of such a fall in the extraordinary discounts that retailers offered during and after the 2008 Christmas shopping season. As the price level declines and expectations of a further decline form, consumers may begin to hoard money, expecting it to buy more in the future. We may be seeing this already—consumers holding back, expecting even greater discounts than were offered during the 2008 Christmas shopping season. (One is hearing it said that "80 percent is the new normal.") Investors may hoard money too, hoping to be able to buy assets more cheaply as prices continue down. There is suspicion that some banks that have received bailout money from the government are doing just that—and also some that have not received bailout money, for the incentive to hoard in order to be able to buy assets at a lower price in the future is not dependent on bailouts. An alternative possibility is that the banks anticipate inflation caused by the government's anti-depression measures and are reluctant to lend high-value dollars now for repayment in cheap dollars later, though they could insist on an interest rate that would vary with inflation, such as one tied to the consumer price index.

If consumers and investors hoard and as a result prices continue falling, credit will dry up almost completely because borrowing in a deflation is expensive even at a zero interest rate. The borrower will be repaying his loan in dollars that will be worth more because they will buy more. Suppose you borrow $1 for a year at a zero interest rate to buy a loaf of bread that is expected to cost only 50 cents in a year. Since $1 will buy two loaves a year from now, in effect you are borrowing one loaf and agreeing to repay the loan with two loaves. That translates into a 100 percent annual interest rate. The example is extreme, but remember that an interest rate has to include a risk premium, and the premium is apt to be very high when one is lending in a depression. So a loan will be very expensive to a borrower even if the deflation rate is moderate.

The effect on employment of a deflation-induced drying-up of credit is likely to be especially acute when a depression has been triggered by the bursting of a housing bubble. Workers will find it difficult to search for jobs far from their home because they will be unable to sell their house without taking a terrific loss. The loss, by erasing their equity, will make it difficult for them to buy a house elsewhere without a big mortgage even though house prices are depressed—and that big mortgage will be prohibitively costly.

The hoarding of cash, which a deflation induces, can make it difficult (or, as we'll see, immensely costly) to stop a deflationary spiral by increasing the money supply. If money does not circulate because people don't want to spend or invest, creating more money will not induce spending or investing. In a deflation the purchasing power of cash grows, which makes putting it under your mattress (or the equivalent) a good investment but exacerbates the deflation. Furthermore, anyone who has debt that he contracted before the deflation will find himself forced to repay it in dollars worth more in purchasing power than the dollars he borrowed. Deflation thus increases a debt burden that is bound to be very heavy already because of the low rate of personal savings and the decline in the value of the assets that people hold as savings. Deflation also aggravates unemployment, as people who lose their jobs lose time searching for jobs that pay the same, because they don't realize at first that a fall in nominal wages need not amount to a fall in real wages.

Eventually deflation will bottom out. As income shrinks, consumers will cease to be able to hoard cash; they will have to start spending everything they have. They won't have much to spend, but then prices will be very low too. As spending picks up, producers will hire more workers, so incomes will rise. A virtuous cycle will be under way. But the process of recovery will be protracted because it will begin from a very low level.

Economists tend to discuss deflation in terms of "liquidity" and "velocity." "Liquidity" we've met before; it refers to cash or something quickly convertible to cash. "Velocity" refers to the rapidity with which money circulates; one can think of it as the number of times in the course of a year that a dollar is used in a transaction; the rest of the time the dollar is idle. A deflation can occur because the demand for liquidity rises, as it is apt to do when people are fearful that they do not have enough savings to tide them over a period of economic stress. They want safety, and cash is safest—indeed during a deflation cash grows in value without having to be invested.

A rise in liquidity causes prices to fall because there is less money available for transactions, and falling prices in turn make holding cash still more desirable. The resulting increase in liquidity (or, equivalently, reduction in velocity) causes prices to fall further unless something is done to increase the amount of money in circulation. Can the Federal Reserve, without causing serious long-term damage to the economy, effectuate an increase in the money supply large enough to prevent prices from falling dangerously? The banking system, currently in distress, is the Federal Reserve's agent in executing monetary policy. And the liquidity preference of banks, other firms, and individuals cannot be gauged in advance.

Economists who think that monetary policy alone can pull us out of our economic doldrums take comfort in a well-known formula for determining the relation of money to prices: $MV = PY$, where M is the amount of money, V its velocity, P the price level, and Y the economy's output. Equivalently, $V = PY/M$—which makes it seem that increasing M must increase economic activity (that is, must increase PY—the market value of the economy's output) in order to maintain the equality between V and PY/M. But this is only because

V is a constant in the equation. If people are fearful of borrowing—if they have a strong liquidity preference—and banks likewise (and banks are therefore reluctant to lend), increasing the money supply may have little or no impact on economic activity. If V is falling at the same rate that M is rising, economic activity will be unaffected by the increase in M. And it may be. As Keynes explained in *The General Theory* (p. 317), "It is the return of confidence, to speak in ordinary language, which is so insusceptible to control in an economy of individualistic capitalism. This is the aspect of the slump which bankers and business men have been right in emphasising, and which the economists who have put their faith in a 'purely monetary' remedy have underestimated."

Bernanke, renowned student that he is of the Great Depression, is terrified of a deflation and determined to prevent it by increasing the money supply by hook or by crook. Buying Treasury bills from banks is unlikely to do the trick, as we saw. But the Federal Reserve is authorized to buy other assets, and it can even buy assets from entities other than banks. Suppose it buys from a bank a bond that pays 6 percent interest. The bank is likely to lend out at least some of the cash that it receives in exchange for the bond, as otherwise it will lose interest revenue that it wanted.

The Federal Reserve has begun buying commercial paper (short-term promissory notes issued by corporations, bypassing banks and other financial intermediaries, in exchange for cash) and other private debt as well, such as credit card debt. The hope is that issuers of these forms of credit will use the cash to issue more credit; for although the demand for credit in general is way down, the demand for particular forms of credit shows signs of life. The Federal Reserve's program of selective purchase of debt resembles the abandoned (or perhaps just suspended) program of buying securitized debt from banks, but differs because the demand for *that* debt had dried up almost completely, with the result that sellers of securitized debt would not use the cash they received from the sale to issue more such debt. The Federal Reserve's program also differs because the securitized debt was opaque, creating acute problems of valuation; the forms of debt that the Fed is now buying are not.

The purchase of private debt, as distinct from the purchase of government securities, is the major use being made of the $800 billion fund created by the Federal Reserve in November 2008 to implement an easy-money program of fighting the depression. Private debt is risky; the Fed will not be able to collect all the private debt that it buys. And maybe it will overpay in order to put that much more cash in circulation, hoping to stimulate buying and lending. That will revive complaints about making gifts of taxpayers' money to the banks. Some conservative economists believe that as long as the Federal Reserve is sufficiently aggressive—even to the point of being hyper-aggressive—in pouring money into the economy, there is no need for the stimulus package; the Fed can do it all—prevent deflation and restore output and employment to their pre-depression levels. The premise of the argument is correct: the demand of banks and individuals for liquidity is not infinite. If the Federal Reserve, say by massive purchase of federal securities from banks, floods the banks with cash, they will begin to lend, and at very low interest rates because there will be *so* much cash available for lending, and consumers will begin to borrow. As for the danger that a massive increase in the money supply will cause a massive increase in inflation after the depression ends, these economists point out that the Federal Reserve can always reverse its expansion of the money supply by selling the securities it has bought from the banks back to them and retiring the cash that it receives from them in exchange for the securities.

But this picture does not seem realistic. (It does not seem realistic to Bernanke, so far as one can judge.) Bank reserves, and therefore the amount of money the banks are allowed to lend, have increased twentyfold in the last eighteen months without stimulating enough lending to eliminate the threat of deflation. Is the answer to increase the banks' reserves another twentyfold, or perhaps fortyfold, or even a hundredfold? Reserves are not what the banks lend (except to each other); they are what determine how much of its capital a bank is permitted to lend. The bank must still find profitable opportunities for lending, and it may not find many in a depression. One reason it may not find any is that the banks—anticipating massive inflation as a result of so enormous an (attempted) expansion in the money supply by the Federal Reserve, and skeptical of whatever assurances the Fed offers that it will clamp down on the money supply the minute the depression ends, and not knowing when that will be—are likely to charge extremely high interest rates, which borrowers, in their currently fearful and necessitous state, will be unwilling to pay.

And if and when the Federal Reserve does reverse its inflationary policy and sells the federal securities that it bought from the banks back to them, there will be a sharp drop in liquidity—a colossal drop, really. The banks will suddenly have so much less cash to lend that just as in 1937, when the Federal Reserve raised interest rates and precipitated the "second depression," and just as when the Federal Reserve broke the inflation of the 1970s with a sharp increase in interest rates (and thus contraction of the supply of money), a severe recession will be unavoidable. In sum, monetary policy alone is unlikely to get us out of the depression at a tolerable cost.

There is an interesting political tension between the monetarist and the Keynesian responses to depression. Both pump money into the economy, the first by the Federal Reserve's buying debt and the second by the Treasury's running a deficit financed by borrowing. The first response, though favored by conservatives (and not only because they prefer Bernanke, a conservative economist, to a Democratic-controlled Congress, which is determining, along with a Democratic President, the size and content of the deficit-spending program), is potentially more socialistic than the second. The Federal

Reserve could end up owning a sizable chunk of the American economy. When the Fed buys and sells federal government securities in order to increase (when it buys them) or reduce (when it sells them) the supply of money for the limited purpose of keeping interest rates within tolerable bounds (in particular not letting them fall so far as to trigger inflation or rise so far as to trigger recession), it is not intervening in particular industries — other than the banking industry, of course. When it starts to buy or sell private debt, it enters private markets directly. It moves from regulating bank credit to providing credit directly, becoming in the process the nation's biggest bank rather than just a regulator of the amount of lending that banks do. (Remember that it is by bank lending that money is created.)

An ominous portent is Citigroup's position on a bill in Congress to authorize bankruptcy judges to rewrite mortgage loans in favor of the mortgagors. That is a strange position for a bank to be advocating. But Citigroup is the recipient of $45 billion in bailout money and a federal guaranty of $300 billion in debt, and the bailout has been much criticized because Citigroup is one of the culprits in the financial crisis. Robert Rubin, a senior executive of Citigroup until his resignation in the wake of the financial crisis, and a senior adviser to Obama's presidential campaign as well, had successfully urged Citigroup to increase its risky lending. Citigroup is too big for its own good (it is about to break up) and poorly managed. Its political position, like that of the Detroit automakers, is highly sensitive. As a major recipient of federal aid—and it may soon ask for more—it can ill afford to resist pressure to support mortgage relief. That would be biting the hand that feeds it. When government gives financial aid to private firms, political strings invariably are attached, especially when the aid is discretionary. The government didn't have to give Citigroup money or guarantee its loans; it could have taken over the company, the way it took over American International Group (in effect), Fannie Mae, and Freddie Mac, or let it die like Lehman Brothers. Not that either result would have been a happy one. Government is no good at running businesses, and we can ill afford the collapse of a bank far larger than Lehman Brothers. But when government starts insuring not only depositors but also the banks themselves, it calls the tune, like any insurer.

The Keynesian response to a depression requires

legislative action and hence has greater democratic legitimacy than actions by the Federal Reserve. But by the same token it is likely to be less disciplined, more politicized—and more liberal. Many of the New Deal programs had no beneficial effect on the economy, and some had a detrimental effect, such as the promotion of cartels by the National Industrial Recovery Act, the promotion of unions by the National Labor Relations Act, and the curtailment of agricultural production by the Agricultural Adjustment Act. Cartels restrict output in order to increase price; unions restrict the supply of labor in order to increase wages; and curtailment of agricultural production reduces output in order to increase the price of farm goods. All three effects reduce rather than increase output and so protract rather than contract a depression. Some economists believe that those programs delayed the recovery from the Great Depression.

The New Deal permanently enlarged American government, for good or for ill. The stimulus program (perhaps it should be called the "half stimulus–half new New Deal" program) is also designed to enlarge the role of government, primarily in the areas of health care, energy policy, and the environment. There is a legitimate concern that

Keynesian depression-fighting theory is being used as a fig leaf to disguise a program of massive government expenditures based on a liberal ideology that a majority of Americans may not subscribe to—at least not yet. That is why conservatives' preferred fiscal solution to a depression is a tax cut rather than a public-works program; it does not enlarge the scope of government—in fact it shrinks it.

Most conservatives, however, would prefer to rely solely on the Federal Reserve to revive the economy by increasing the supply of money. But we have seen that that may not work. You can lead a bank to money but you cannot make it lend any more than you can make a person borrow, and if there is no bank lending (or very little) the purchase of bank assets by the Federal Reserve will not lift the economy out of a depression—it may not even prevent a deflation. And we have just seen that a maximum effort by the Federal Reserve to prevent deflation by expanding the money supply could produce horrendous side effects. This is why most economists, including many who until a few months ago were anti-Keynesian Friedmanite monetarists, have come to favor, however grudgingly, some sort of deficit-spending program to supplement, and by supplementing limit, Bernanke's aggressive use of monetary policy to avoid deflation and speed economic recovery. Bernanke himself is a conservative, a monetarist; his support of deficit spending signifies a loss of faith in the adequacy of monetarist cures for depressions.

Even supposing that the stimulus will do nothing to speed recovery from the depression, there would still be a compelling argument for it, though not an argument that economists have tools to evaluate. Suppose that President Obama were to tell the American public: "We're trying to avert or ameliorate a depression by pumping up the money supply, but it may not work, in which event we'll find ourselves in a deflationary spiral that may resemble what happened to the United States in the 1930s and Japan in the 1990s. And then we'll just have to tough it out because our toolbox will be empty." (This is what, in effect, some conservative economists would like him to say.) His statement would guarantee a severe depression, because people would react by curtailing their consumption further, accelerating a deflationary spiral that would carry the economy to a lower level and keep it there for years. The people would not be responding to the statement with irrational panic, but merely placing appropriate weight on a credible statement by the respected head of government.

It is better to maintain a modicum of public optimism by statements of confidence backed up by commitments to expensive public programs even though the programs may well fail, or more likely achieve much less than was hoped for. That is one reason the $819 billion stimulus proposal has not been subjected to a cost-benefit analysis. Another is that a depression is a political as well as an economic event and that every major act of government is political. But the biggest reason is lack of information. Neither economists nor business forecasters can tell us with any confidence how far the economic downturn would go if there were no further government intervention, what the social costs of that steeper downturn would be, and what the effectiveness and long-term costs of various types and levels of intervention would be. Without all these numbers it is impossible to determine the economically optimal course of action. What the government does to fight the depression will be based on a combination of economic guesswork and political expediency. The absence of contingency planning by government officials and academic economists has left no alternative to this seat-of-the-pants approach.

Some of the responses to the depression that are being contemplated, and that at this writing are rapidly gaining momentum, don't quite fit the categories that I have been using. Mainly they are proposals to help homeowners who have seen the value of their houses decline precipitously. They may have bought their homes with proceeds of a mortgage loan that required no payment of interest for the first two years, and the two years are now up. They may face deficiency judgments if they default and their mortgage is foreclosed, because the unpaid balance of the mortgage exceeds the resale value of the house. The decline in housing prices has been so precipitous that many people who bought a house at the peak of the bubble have lost their principal savings—the house—which may make it very difficult for them to move elsewhere, for example to find a job. And they may be unable to renegotiate their mortgage with the mortgage-service company that administers it because the servicer is the agent of principals who have conflicting interests—owners of the different risk tiers of a mortgage-backed security.

Let me dwell on the last point for a moment.

The modification of a mortgage loan that is straining the mortgagor's ability to pay may avert a default and by doing so assure that the owners of the top tier of a mortgage-backed security will be repaid in full. But it may wipe out some of the owners of the lower tiers. So the terms of the security itself or some notion of fiduciary duty may oblige the servicer to obtain the unanimous consent of the owners of the different tiers (which would require compensating the owners of the lower tiers—a requirement of unanimity empowers holdouts) in order to be entitled to modify one of these mortgages in the pool of mortgages that backs the security, and this will increase the transaction costs of modification.

An economic-legal team at Columbia University has proposed that to facilitate modification and thus reduce the foreclosure rate, Congress should pass a law that would allow the mortgage servicer to modify a mortgage without the consent of all the owners but would provide government compensation for the lower-tier investors. There would be a net social gain because the mortgagor would have a little more money and the value of the securitized debt would be greater, since foreclosure creates deadweight losses.

It is a better proposal than the proposal that is being pushed in Congress to amend Chapter 13 of the Bankruptcy Code to allow bankruptcy judges to "cram down" first mortgages on primary residences. To explain, in an ordinary Chapter 13 bankruptcy (a counterpart, for bankrupt individuals, to corporate reorganization) the bankruptcy judge can reduce ("cram down") secured debts owed by the bankrupt. A creditor who has a lien (that is, a secured interest) can still enforce it but the amount by which the debt exceeds the value of the lien can be converted to an unsecured debt. If the bankrupt owes $20,000 secured by a lien on his car, and the lien is worth $5,000, the bankruptcy judge can convert $15,000 of the loan to an unsecured claim, which like other unsecured debts will probably be worth only a few cents on the dollar in bankruptcy.

Under present law, a bankruptcy judge cannot cram down a mortgage on a person's primary residence, and the push is to change that law. Suppose you have a $500,000 mortgage on a house that has lost value and is now worth only $300,000. With cram-down the mortgage would be reduced to $300,000 and the remaining amount you owe would be converted to an unsecured debt that, like other unsecured debt, could be both reduced and stretched out in bankruptcy. If the owner could keep up his diminished mortgage payments, the mortgagee could not foreclose. So allowing cram-down would be a genuine measure of mortgage relief. It would also burden the bankruptcy courts, reward a number of feckless bubble buyers, establish a precedent that would encourage future housing bubbles, and increase interest rates on mortgages by reducing mortgagees' legal remedies—and higher interest rates would retard the refinancing of mortgages and the purchase of houses. Even the benefits in terms of mortgage relief (but also the costs) would be small, because even homeowners who would benefit from a cram-down of their mortgage would be reluctant to seek it. They would have to declare Chapter 13 bankruptcy. And in a Chapter 13 bankruptcy you cannot just kiss your debts goodbye; you are required to dedicate a significant portion of your current and future income to repaying as many of them as possible.

A better idea for mortgage relief (besides the Columbia proposal) might be a moratorium on foreclosures. The analogy would be to the "automatic stay" in bankruptcy. When a firm declares bankruptcy, its creditors are automatically enjoined from trying to collect the debts they are owed by the bankrupt. The reason is to prevent a premature liquidation, which might result if each creditor were permitted to grab as much of the bankrupt's assets as he could ahead of the other creditors, since there will not be enough to go around (otherwise the debtor would not be bankrupt). Similarly, the efforts of mortgage-service companies to foreclose their mortgages all at once are producing a glut of houses for sale at foreclosure sales, and this may be driving the price of housing below its long-run equilibrium value, especially since the sales are being made during a depression. A temporary freeze on foreclosures would facilitate the renegotiation of troubled mortgages and the sale of homes at a more leisurely pace.

Congress could probably go further and cut down the mortgages themselves. I say "probably" because undoubtedly such a measure would be challenged on constitutional grounds. Not as a taking—an exercise of the eminent domain power—for which just compensation would have to be paid, because the government would not be "taking" the mortgage in the sense of becoming the mortgagee. But a mortgage is a form of property, and the due process clause of the Fifth Amendment forbids the federal government to deprive a person of property without due process of law. "Due process" is a vague concept, however, and if the government could show a compelling interest for cutting down a mortgagee's property right, the courts would probably allow it to do so. Likewise with a law that eliminated, with or without compensation, the right of owners of junior tiers of mortgage-backed securities to block modification of the underlying mortgages.

My politically incorrect inclination would be to oppose all forms of mortgage relief; implementation would be complex and costly and the net contribution to fighting the depression probably slight. My reaction is part of a broader concern, articulated in subsequent chapters, that a depression is not the right time for regulatory innovations beyond the bare minimum essential for recovering from the depression.

6

A Silver Lining?

THE COSTS of a depression in lost output, reduced incomes, wasteful government spending, burdensome public debt, future inflation, a recession to choke off the inflation, property crimes (including arson of overinsured properties), and anxiety are sure to exceed the benefits and can even lead to disastrous political consequences. Had it not been for the Great Depression, Hitler might not have become chancellor of Germany. Depressions, even recessions, have had political consequences in the United States as well—the election of Franklin Roosevelt in 1932 and of Bill Clinton in 1992, and Barack Obama's margin of victory and the strengthening of Democratic control of Congress in 2008—but as yet no disastrous consequences. Of course all three of *these* examples might be thought positive consequences of an economic downturn—and this is appropriate to note because my objective in this chapter is to try to cheer up the reader by pointing out that a depression can have good consequences as well as bad, even if the latter preponderate.

To begin with, a depression backs up efforts to moderate the business cycle. The housing bubble could not expand indefinitely; leverage could not keep growing indefinitely. When the ratio of borrowed to equity capital reaches 35 to 1—Bear Stearns' ratio when it collapsed (and UBS's reached 50 to 1)—a mere 3 percent fall in the value of the firm's assets will plunge the firm into insolvency. The government was doing nothing to prick the bubble and too little to keep leverage within safe bounds. The longer the world economy went without a depression, the worse the collapse would be when it finally, inevitably, came.

Warren Buffett is reported to have said that you don't know who's swimming naked until the tide goes out. The receding stock market tide exposed Bernard Madoff, who is said to have confessed to having pulled off the biggest Ponzi scheme in history. The scheme would have lasted longer and the losses to investors would have been greater had the stock market crash been postponed. The crash reduced the value of Madoff's hedge fund, but more important (because the fund probably had little in the way of assets), the general economic collapse caused requests for redemptions of investments in hedge funds and other investment funds to soar, and Madoff could not honor his investors' requests for redemption and as a result his scheme collapsed. It is another example of the fragility of the banking industry; without insurance of loans made to banks in the form of demand deposits or otherwise, banks are subject to runs.

A depression increases the efficiency with which both labor and capital inputs are used by business, because it creates an occasion and an imperative for reducing slack. One might think that a firm that has slack in good times will have as much incentive to reduce it as it would in bad times; slack (failing to maximize profits) is an opportunity cost, which in classical economic theory has the same motivational effect as an out-of-pocket expense. But firms are organizations, and organizations incur "agency costs," which are more difficult to control in good times than in bad. Principal and agent (for example, employer and employee) often have divergent objectives, and to the extent that the agent is able to pursue his own objectives he will be imposing costs on his principal. The problem of executive overcompensation, which I discussed in an earlier chapter, is thus a problem of agency costs.

If a firm's profits are growing, the firm's executives will find it easier to skim off some of the profits, pocketing them in the form of excessive compensation or perquisites (private aircraft, flowers in the executive dining room, etc.), than when the firm is shrinking. In the former case stockholders will be doing well—will have no sense of grievance, of being ripped off by management—so the pressure (weak as it is at best) that they exert through the board of directors to minimize the diversion of profits to executives and other employees, and other wasteful activities condoned when shareholders are happy, will be less intense than when the firm is at risk of collapsing. In the latter case, the executives themselves will have a strong incentive to minimize costs, including, in extreme cases, their own compensation. When a depression ends, a firm motivated by the depression to reduce slack in its operations will have lower average costs than before, though they will drift upward as the firm regrows.

Similarly, the depression should induce states, cities, and the federal government, all of which are experiencing sharply reduced tax revenues, to provide public services more efficiently. It will accelerate the desirable trend toward privatization of government services, such as toll roads and airports. Conservatives fear that the depression will have the opposite effect, that of encouraging the growth of government beyond what economic prosperity requires. They may be right—but I am trying to look on the bright side. And one bright spot is the beating that the United Auto Workers has taken in the court of public opinion. The UAW has been called the parasite that kills its host—or, to change the metaphor, the dinosaur union battling the dinosaur automakers, with all being slated for extinction. That is too harsh a condemnation. But the long-term decline of adversarial unions, as distinct from unions that focus on common interests of labor and management, such as increasing workplace safety and protecting workers from abusive superiors (a company's imperfect control of its supervisory employees is another example of agency costs), has enhanced productivity. The UAW's role in the decline of the Detroit auto industry underscores the potential dangers to the economy, in a period of great economic stress, of Democrats' traditional fondness for unions, which stems from the efforts that unions make to get Democratic politicians elected, as well as from New Deal nostalgia and other forms of sentimental liberalism.

Quite apart from the UAW, the depression may give the Administration and Congress pause concerning measures to strengthen unions, such as the proposed Employee Free Choice Act. The act would abolish the requirement of secret elections to determine whether a workplace shall be unionized and, if the union prevails and union and employer cannot agree on the terms of a collective bargaining agreement, would require binding arbitration. A fall in wages is a problem in a depression, as we know, because it can further a deflationary spiral, although it can also reduce unemployment, so that the net effect is uncertain. But an increase in wages, and a reduction in the efficiency with which labor is utilized (because of union-imposed work rules), will have an unambiguously negative effect on output by increasing employers' labor costs, and the reduction in output will lead to an increase in unemployment. The National Labor Relations Act was, we recall, a New Deal union-promoting measure regarded by some economists as a factor in delaying the recovery from the Great Depression.

Even though by undermining faith in free markets the depression is opening the door to more government intervention in the economy and eventually to higher taxes (though not until the economy improves), these are not *necessarily* bad things, although they can be, as we have just seen. Obviously neither the optimal amount of government intervention nor the optimal amount of taxation is zero, and how small they should be is unclear. I have already suggested that there is a range of unmet social needs that only government can meet. Although in principle most of the money needed for them could be obtained by cutting wasteful government programs, considerations of political feasibility limit the amount of economizing that can be achieved.

Federal tax rates are lower today than they were in the 1940s, 1950s, and 1960s—periods of healthy economic growth. The top marginal income tax rate reached 94 percent in 1945 and did not decline to 70 percent until 1965 (it is 35 percent today). A modest increase in marginal rates from their present low level would increase tax revenues substantially, probably with little offset due to the distortions that any tax produces. And it would reduce executive overcompensation, which I have argued is one of the practices that helped precipitate the financial crisis. But the bulk of any feasible augmentation of tax revenues will have to be devoted to paying down the depression-enhanced national debt, leaving little for other public needs. So our government probably will remain pretty small by international standards.

By increasing unemployment, a depression increases the demand for education. It does this by reducing opportunity cost—forgone income is the largest cost of higher education to a student. Education produces benefits for the entire society. Educated people are more productive than uneducated ones yet cannot capture the entire product of their efforts in the form of a higher income. (For example, a patent expires after twenty years, allowing the patented product or process to be used by anybody without compensation to the inventor.) It might seem that a depression would also reduce the income gains from being educated and so the incentive to become educated. But as those gains accrue over a lifetime, they are little affected by a depression during a person's school years.

A depression is a learning experience. The banking industry has certainly learned a great deal from the current financial crisis about the risks of leverage and the downside of complex financial instruments intended to reduce the risk of default more cheaply than by traditional means (means such as having extra-large reserves to buffer any unexpected decline in a bank's loan revenues). The public has been taught a lesson about the dangers of speculating on housing prices and investing the rest of one's savings in the stock market, where they are at risk.

History suggests, however, that such lessons are quickly forgotten. There is therefore merit in a suggestion by the finance theorist Luigi Zingales that a high-level ad hoc committee, public or private, be appointed to conduct a thoroughgoing Warren Commission or 9/11 Commission type of inquiry into the management of the economy over the past decade, culminating in the frenzied efforts of Bernanke and Paulson in the fall of 2008 to stave off a depression. We need to have a clear idea of what they thought they were doing, what information they acted on, whom they consulted and why, and what the consequences have been. And then it may be possible to devise ways of preventing a recurrence.

The depression has shown that privatizing social security—that is, allowing recipients to invest in the stock market some or all of the money in their social security retirement accounts—would have been calamitous. The depression has also had an important noneducative consequence: it has driven down commodity prices. Of particular importance has been its dramatic effect on the price of oil, which has nose-dived in the last six months. The price spike in the spring of 2008 seems to have been due primarily to a belief that the industry could not expand production fast enough to keep pace with surging demand, particularly in China and India, and the fall in price seems due to the worldwide reduction in demand for oil caused by the global depression. The combination of low prices of oil with low demand for oil is optimal from the standpoint of U.S. (and probably world) welfare. The low demand reduces the level of carbon emissions, thus alleviating, if only slightly, the problem of global warming. And the fall in price has reduced the wealth of the oil-producing nations—a goal that should be central to U.S. foreign policy because so many of those nations are either hostile to the United States (notably Russia, Iran, and Venezuela) or politically unstable (such as Iraq, Nigeria, and Algeria).

The excessive borrowing that precipitated the current depression enabled, for a period of years, higher personal consumption expenditures than the nation could afford. Thus the current drop in consumption is in part just an offset to the abnormal level of consumption earlier. Because people loaded up with cars, electronic gear, clothes, etc. while times were good (illusorily good, because the nation was living beyond its means), the current reduction in the purchase of durable goods, while hard on sellers, may not be a great hardship to consumers. But it will be at least a small hardship; people quickly get habituated to a high level of consumption, and a decline from that level is painful. And then there are the people who didn't load up with consumer durables during the boom and now cannot afford to buy them because their income has dropped.

The depression will reduce the recruitment of brilliant people to work for financial firms. The reason this might be a good thing lies in the difference between private and social returns to labor. Teachers, scientists, and inventors are examples of workers who provide benefits to others that exceed, on average, the providers' monetary incomes. Probably this is also true of highly paid entertainers, but not of financial executives who rake in many millions, sometimes hundreds of millions, of dollars every year. Not that the proper management of credit is unimportant to the American economy; it is enormously important, as the depression has shown. But it does not follow that Harvard Ph.D.'s in high-energy physics contribute more to society by working for hedge funds, as many of them do, along with other men and women who have outstanding quantitative skills, than they would contribute in other jobs for which they are qualified that pay less. The depression in finance will channel some of these people into less lucrative but socially more productive jobs.

The depression is a wake-up call to the economics profession. The profession's failure to foresee the depression, and its unpreparedness to suggest timely, effective responses to it, will stimulate fresh thinking in macroeconomics and financial economics. It may even lead to a merger between depression economics, a branch of macroeconomics, and finance viewed as a distinct field of economics (much as statistics is a distinct field of mathematics). Recessions precipitated by a banking crisis are more likely than other recessions to turn into depressions because of the severe negative effect of a breakdown in the credit system on personal consumption expenditures, an effect that sets the stage for deflation. Macroeconomists are the experts on recessions and depressions, finance theorists on the operation of the financial system. The latter were quicker to spot the storm clouds. The former are chastened not only by their failures of foresight and understanding but also by finding themselves uncertain about how to place the economy on the path to recovery. A closer integration of the two disciplines might have enabled earlier and more decisive responses to the downturn.

The depression may have paid for itself, as it were, if it leads to a durable increase in the personal savings rate. The experience of the depression should induce greater thrift, which will increase the formation of investment capital after the depression abates so that we don't continue living off our rich uncles China, Japan, and Germany, who provide us with all sorts of goods in exchange for our currency. But there is a more important reason that we need a higher rate of personal savings. We need it in order to adjust to the aging of the population. The longer people live, the more consumption they must shift forward to their retirement years, and so the more money they must save when they are young if they are to finance their own retirement rather than be a burden on their children and the taxpayer. True, they can work longer as their longevity increases, but probably not proportionately longer; and even if they can, expenditures on health care increase with age, and thus underscore the need for people to shift their consumption expenditures forward in time by consuming less, and therefore saving more, when young. The more that people save, the less pressure there will be on government to finance personal consumption expenditures through programs like social security and Medicare. Those programs should supplement rather than replace personal savings.

Even deflation has a silver lining, though a very small one. In a deflation, as we know, a person can earn interest just by leaving his money in his safe deposit box (or under his mattress, for that matter)—he doesn't have to bother dealing with a money market fund. That is a real cost savings, and is the basis on which Milton Friedman proposed that the Federal Reserve set a rate of monetary expansion slightly below the rate of growth in output, so that the currency would deflate at a predictable rate. The *expected* discount rate is critical; the higher it is, the likelier are cash hoarding and the other pathologies that deflation can cause.

7

What We Are Learning
about Capitalism and Government

CAPITALISM WILL SURVIVE the current depression as it did the Great Depression of the 1930s. It will survive because there is no alternative that hasn't been thoroughly discredited, which wasn't as clear in the 1930s. It is clear now. The Soviet, Maoist, "corporatist" (fascist Italy), Cuban, Venezuelan, etc. alternatives to capitalism are unappealing, to say the least. Yet capitalism may survive only in a compromised form—think of the spur that the Great Depression gave to collectivism. Spawned in the depression, the New Deal ushered in a long era of heavy-handed government regulation of the economy; and likewise today there is both advocacy and the actuality of renewed regulation and an impending increase in the size of government. Hence the importance of the question whether government may have been responsible for the current crisis. For if so this would be a powerful argument against reregulation—against the new New Deal that liberal economists like Paul Krugman and Joseph Stiglitz are dreaming of—though not an argument that would have much political traction during the present emergency.

I have already indicated my doubts that the government bears the basic responsibility for causing the depression. As far as one can judge on the basis of what is known today (obviously an important qualification), the depression is the result of normal business activity in a laissez-faire economic regime—more precisely, it is an event consistent with the normal operation of economic markets. Bankers and consumers alike seem on the whole to have been acting in conformity with their rational self-interest throughout the period that saw the increase in risky banking practices, the swelling and bursting of the housing bubble, and a reduction in the rate of personal savings combined with an increase in the riskiness of those savings. The market participants made plenty of mistakes, but that is par for the course. Whenever has it been different? Economic life is permeated with uncertainty.

The media are having a field day exposing instances of financiers' malfeasance, misfeasance, folly, and seemingly egregious extravagance. Sometimes they misunderstand what they denounce. An example is the thunder of criticism of John Thain's $1.2 million redecoration of his office suite when he became CEO of Merrill Lynch, months before Merrill Lynch's swoon into the arms of Bank America. Companies that raise billions of dollars, some of it from immensely wealthy investors, have a legitimate business interest in decorating their quarters in a manner apt to impress such investors. The financial crisis was indeed the consequence of decisions, some mistaken, by financiers. But the mistakes were systemic—the product of the nature of the banking business in an environment shaped by low interest rates and deregulation rather than the antics of crooks and fools.

Laissez-faire capitalism failed us, but government allowed the preconditions of depression to develop and wreak havoc with the economy. And its responses to the crisis were late, slow, indecisive, and poorly articulated. The responses also created "moral hazard" (the tendency to engage in risky behavior if one is insured against the consequences of the risks' materializing). They did this by eliminating the limits on federal deposit insurance of bank deposits and by extending that insurance to checkable accounts in money market funds, but more important by bailing out failing firms deemed "too big to fail"—an incentive for corporate giantism and financial irresponsibility (which go hand in hand because the difficulty of controlling subordinates grows with the size of an organization). The government gratuitously disrupted the operations of hedge funds by limiting short selling—at the height of the banking crisis the Securities and Exchange Commission forbade short selling of financial stocks. And by substantially increasing the federal deficit, the government's responses to the crisis are sowing the seeds of a future inflation. But of these criticisms, the main ones— the creation of moral hazard and the planting of the seeds of a future inflation—concern the unavoidable side effects of any effective measures to limit a depression.

To blame the government for the depression is questionable in two respects. First, were there no government regulation of the economy, there probably would still have been a depression, because even without the Federal Reserve's loose monetary policy in the early 2000s there would have been enough capital from abroad to keep interest rates low unless the Fed had been more alert than it was to the risk of depression that low interest rates create. And remember that other factors contributed to the financial crisis that brought on the depression besides low interest rates: aggressive marketing of mortgages, a widespread appetite for risk, a highly competitive, largely deregulated finance industry, and debt securitization.

Businessmen and individuals would, it is true, have been more cautious had there been no prospect of government bailouts (that is the moral-hazard issue). Although bailouts do not save all firms, all careers, or all shareholder values, firms that are saved by a bailout retain employees who would have lost their jobs had the firm not been saved, and equity values are preserved that would disappear in bankruptcy. Still, a bailout is a traumatic experience. Even holders of secure debt are often badly hurt, because the value of their collateral falls. But overriding moral-hazard concerns is the fact that depressions would be significantly deeper and last significantly longer were government unwilling to take aggressive steps to counter them with monetary and fiscal measures.

Second, in financial regulation the line between government and the private sector is blurred. This was especially true in the Bush Administration.

Bernanke and Paulson are neither politicians nor career civil servants, though Bernanke has spent the last six years in government, Paulson only the last two (and he's gone now), after a career as an investment banker. Their principal advisers have (in Paulson's case had) been investment bankers and academic economists rather than career employees of the Federal Reserve and the Treasury, though with the important exception of Timothy Geithner, who before becoming Treasury Secretary in the Obama Administration was the president of the Federal Reserve Bank of New York. Even the temporary prohibition of short selling of financial stocks, which might seem to reflect the kind of mindless hostility to speculation that one expects from politicians, was strongly urged by the CEO of Morgan Stanley and by other financiers. The White House, the Congress, and the *faitnéant* Securities and Exchange Commission were bit players in the anti-depression measures that the Bush Administration took with its expiring breath. In effect, the government's power to repair the crisis that Wall Street created was delegated to Wall Street.

Not that it was an innovation of the Bush Administration to recruit the top financial officials of government from the financial sector and academia. But it is notable how recently Bernanke and Paulson had been appointed, how heavily they relied for advice in fighting the depression on financial experts from the private sector, and how small a role the politicians in Congress and the White House played. Congress made a lot of noise but in the end rubber-stamped most of the proposals made by Bernanke and Paulson, though partly because most of the responses to the depression were made during a lame-duck Congress. Ironically, the new top-heavy Democratic Congress is likely to be more assertive, indeed more restive, under the new Democratic President than it was under his Republican predecessor. A President of the same party that controls Congress feels less need to cajole and flatter the members of his party, and also likes to reduce his dependence on them by building bridges to the legislators of the other party. This threatens the power of the legislators of his own party and injures their *amour propre*, and they fight back.

I do not criticize the delegation of the handling of a financial crisis to financial experts rather than to politicians and bureaucrats. But it is further evidence that the financial crisis is indeed a crisis of capitalism rather than a failure of government.

Conservatives like to beat up on Fannie Mae and Freddie Mac—the federally sponsored companies that own or insure a large fraction of the nation's mortgages and are among the financial enterprises whose risky practices contributed to the crisis. Fannie Mae invented mortgage-backed securities, though it backed the securities that it issued only with prime mortgages. Both companies got entangled with the lower-grade mortgage-backed securities and were collapsing in September 2008 and were taken over by the government. But although federally chartered, they were until then private corporations. Had they not had shareholders and highly compensated managers, they would not have taken as many risks as they did because they would not have had the same profit opportunities. Their behavior mirrored that of the banking industry as a whole, which is no surprise given their private character.

Conservatives also claim that the Community Reinvestment Act of 1977, and amendments made to it in the 1990s, contributed to the financial crisis. The act requires the federal bank regulatory authorities to encourage banks to lend money to people who are poor credit risks because they have modest incomes. Other legislation passed in the

1990s encouraged Fannie Mae and Freddie Mac to increase the number of mortgage loans to low- and middle-income families that it guarantees. But the laws did not actually *require* the banks to make risky loans, and there is a lack of convincing evidence that the laws were responsible for a substantial amount of the risky lending made during the housing bubble.

These laws were part of a broader effort by the Clinton and (second) Bush Administrations to pressure lenders to relax mortgage standards in order to expand homeownership. Regulated firms, including banks, cannot just thumb their noses at politicians and civil servants. But the pressure exerted by the government to lower lending standards was a case of pushing on an open door, if my analysis of the underlying causes of the financial crisis is sound. Banks *wanted* to make risky mortgage loans.

The critical role of government in the crisis was one of permission rather than of encouragement. By having over a period of decades largely deregulated banking, and credit generally, the government inadvertently allowed the rational self-interested decisions of private actors—bankers, mortgage brokers, real estate salesmen, homeowners, and others—to bring on a financial crisis that the government was unable to prevent from molting into a depression. A profound failure of the market was abetted by governmental inaction. That inaction was the result in part of political pressures (to keep interest rates down, to maintain the illusion of prosperity, and to conciliate powerful political interests that are—not incidentally—large contributors to political campaigns). But it was also a result of complacency on the part of government officials and the natural assumption that those officials had acquired effective tools for preventing a depression; seventy-five years after the Great Depression reached bottom in March 1933, no one expected a repetition—depressions were "history." The government's inaction was also the product of a free-market ideology shared to a considerable extent by the Clinton Administration, and for that matter predecessor administrations going back to the 1970s, when the movement to deregulate the financial industry began. This ideological commitment was carried to new heights by the Bush Administration and is typified by the SEC's failure to detect the Madoff swindle.

The swindle, which came to light in December 2008, was a by-product of the depression rather than a cause, yet it has made the depression worse by casting a shadow over an important example of private regulation: the financial institutions known as "funds of funds." These are hedge funds that invest in other hedge funds or in similar investment funds and justify the fees they charge their investors as compensation for choosing the best hedge funds in which to invest (there are thousands of hedge funds) and monitoring their performance. Hedge funds are secretive; the funds of funds operate, or claim to operate, as a kind of private Securities and Exchange Commission supervising the hedge fund industry. But it seems that some of the funds of funds invested in Madoff's Ponzi scheme without performing the kind of "due diligence" that their customers had been led to expect. If the confidence of the investment community in the vigilance of the funds of funds is shaken, this will cause additional requests by customers of hedge funds to withdraw their money.

But the aspect of the Madoff scandal that I want to emphasize is the light it sheds on a philosophy of government that contributed to the depression. This fascinating swindle of apparently unprecedented scope had been going on for decades, yet it had not been detected by the Securities and Exchange Commission, even though, beginning eight years ago, a money manager named Harry Markopolos had bombarded the commission with accusations that Madoff was operating a Ponzi scheme. In this common type of fraud, the investor usually is promised a ridiculously high return on his investment—10 percent a month would not be unusual. The initial investors are paid as promised, though unbeknownst to them out of their own principal and the principal of the other investors. Their happy-seeming experience, spread through word of mouth, encourages others to invest, and the newcomers' investments, used to pay the promised returns both to themselves and to the original investors, keeps the scheme going. Eventually it collapses and the schemer absconds with the money that he has retained rather than paid out in purported earnings on the investments, though at this writing it is unclear what happened to the money invested with Madoff.

Madoff's scheme as described in the media (there has not yet been a judicial hearing on the accusations against him, and I offer no comment on his legal situation) was unique in size and duration. His reputation in the securities industry as a pioneer in electronic trading, and his status as a former chairman of NASDAQ, enabled him to attract sophisticated investors with the assurance of returns that were moderate (about 10 percent a year) in Ponzi terms, but steady. No sophisticated investor would invest with someone who promised 10 percent a month. The typical Ponzi schemer is a charming con man who dangles promises of instant wealth before suckers. The more moderate the returns promised by the Ponzi schemer, the longer the scheme can survive the loss of capital caused by the schemer's paying his investors their promised returns out of principal that is not earning what has been promised.

Some journalists, confusing Ponzi schemes with pyramid schemes, have described the housing and credit bubbles as Ponzi schemes. That is inaccurate. The essence of a Ponzi scheme is deception. The investor thinks that the promised high return on his investment will come from the promoter's putting the investment to work, not that his investment will be used to pay other investors in order to keep the scheme going. There need be no deception in a pyramid scheme, as where a person pays a fee to become a retail seller of a manufacturer's product and is promised a share of the fee of any other retail seller whom he recruits. Eventually there are no more recruits, and that is like what happens in a speculative bubble, which must eventually stop expanding and then burst. But in neither case is there deception—or irrationality. A pyramid scheme is a form of gambling. A bubble is not, if investors have a reasonable expectation of a continued increase in value. Remember that it is only after the bubble bursts that a run up in prices can be said for sure to have been a bubble.

A minimally energetic investigation of Markopolos's accusations would have revealed that Madoff's volume of trading was too small to generate the profits that he was reporting to his investors or to execute the hedge that he claimed kept those profits steady. Yet the Securities and Exchange Commission remained in the dark until it learned along with everyone else that he had been arrested. Conservatives say, what can you expect?—for they believe that regulation is hopelessly inefficient and it should be up to investors to protect themselves as best they can against securities frauds. The SEC's budget was increased substantially between 2002 and 2003 in reaction to the commission's having failed to detect the Enron, WorldCom, and other frauds that had come to light in the early years of the new century, yet it still failed to detect Madoff's scheme.

An alternative hypothesis that seems more plausible than sheer, immutable regulatory ineptitude is that the emphatically pro-business philosophy of the Bush Administration made the SEC too trusting of the securities industry. Markets were believed to be self-regulating, so the Securities and Exchange Commission could go to sleep. And go to sleep it did. Its last chairman during Bush's presidency, Christopher Cox, has been roundly criticized for shrinking, undermining, and demoralizing the commission's enforcement staff—and even its risk-assessment office. Just days before the collapse of Bear Stearns marked the beginning of the acute phase of the financial crisis, Cox declared: "We have a good deal of comfort about the capital cushions at these firms at the moment." Most of the firms about which he was speaking—the investment banks—were teetering on the brink of insolvency; some of them were already over the brink.

The government's regulatory failure was great, but it cannot extenuate the market's failure. More precisely, it cannot conceal—indeed it highlights—the need for better government regulation to secure the public good of financial stability. Not that the government was entirely passive. The very low interest rates of the early 2000s were a product of deliberate government policy, and they encouraged banks to increase their leverage. But the existence of an opportunity is not the same thing as the decision to exploit it. Nothing forces a lender to increase its leverage when interest rates fall. The firm can instead add equity in proportion as it borrows more, to maintain the same debt-equity ratio. The banks had to *decide* to increase their leverage, and they should not be allowed to shift the responsibility for that decision to the government ("deregulation made me do it"), any more than they should be allowed to blame the financial instruments, such as mortgage-backed securities and credit-default swaps, that seemed to reduce the riskiness of leverage. Those instruments were developed in, believed in, and acted on by the private sector. The banks decided to take risks that could and did bring about an economic catastrophe. But whether "blame" is the right response to even a catastrophic market failure is a separate question, which I discuss in chapter 9, from whether industry or government was more responsible in a causal sense.

However the issue of relative responsibility is resolved, there undoubtedly was a grave government failure as well as a market failure, and the standard political responses to a major governmental failure are regulation and reorganization. The latter often takes priority over the former. The government wants to prove that it is doing something to prevent a repetition, and the cheapest yet most visible and dramatic way to show that it has "gotten the message" and is "doing something" is to reorganize. Hence the creation of the Department of Homeland Security and the Directorate of National Intelligence in the wake of the 9/11 attacks. A plausible though probably erroneous case was made that consolidation would close gaps in the protection of the nation against terrorist attacks and other calamities. A similar but more compelling case can be made for consolidation of the multiplicity of federal agencies that regulate the financial system; and it is beginning to seem likely that there will be such a reorganization. If in the course of it the Securities and Exchange Commission is abolished as punishment for its inaction, Bernard Madoff and Christopher Cox can share the credit.

But to reorganize in the midst of crisis, and likewise to regulate or reregulate in the midst of crisis, is a formula for chaos. The argument for doing either is that the ability to change the institutional structure of financial regulation will fade with time; the President's power is at its maximum now, and should be used, and doubtless will be. But as I will argue in chapter 10, the question of how best to regulate financial intermediation is far too difficult to be answered intelligently in haste by government officials preoccupied with the here-and-now problems of fighting a depression. Indeed the main effect of trying to overhaul the system of financial regulation is likely to be to prolong the depression by distracting the officials from their efforts to revive the economy and by making the business environment of the banks and other financial intermediaries even more uncertain than it now is. At least the Bush Administration waited until the 9/11 attacks ended before creating the Department of Homeland Security and the Directorate of National Intelligence. A restructuring of the immensely complex financial sector should await, if not the end of the depression, at least the beginning of the end.

8

The Economics Profession
Asleep at the Switch

ONE OF THE BIGGEST PUZZLES about the failure to anticipate the financial crisis is the lack of foresight of so many academic economists. There were exceptions; Nouriel Roubini was only the most emphatic of the Cassandras. Raghuram Rajan issued strong warnings in 2005, Paul Krugman in the summer of 2007, Martin Feldstein that fall. I mentioned Robert Shiller. The collapse of Bear Stearns in March 2008 elicited warnings from other economists, such as Alan Blinder and Lawrence Summers—the latter of whom, however, had sarcastically dismissed Rajan's warnings three years earlier as "leaden-eyed." But as far as I know, only Roubini among prominent academic economists forecast an actual depression. Warnings about recession do not attract much attention, and perhaps should not. The standard response to a recession is for the Federal Reserve to lower interest rates. That is what it did in response to the mild post-9/11 recession—thus setting the stage for the credit binge that has precipitated a depression.

Macroeconomics and financial economics are highly prestigious fields of economics, and the leading macroeconomists and finance theorists are brilliant people. Yet although the housing bubble started to leak air in 2005 and burst in 2006 and the economy was in recession from the end of 2007 at the latest and the drumbeat of signals warning of an impending crash became deafening by the spring of 2008, not enough economists, whether in academia, the government, or business, sounded the alarm in time to have a significant impact on the government or the banking industry. Securitization of mortgages and other debts was taken at face value as protecting us against the kind of housing-credit bubbles that had ravished East Asian countries in the 1990s. In May 2006, Federal Reserve chairman Bernanke said that the housing market was "cooling," but that this cooling was "orderly and moderate" and that the market appeared to be "headed for a safe landing." His predecessor, Alan Greenspan, who in July 2005 had expressed mild concern about housing prices, said in October 2006 that the "worst may well be over." Public officials cannot be expected to be completely candid at all times. But the statements by Greenspan and Bernanke that I have quoted in this book were misleading; they made things worse.

In September 2007, Robert Lucas said that he was "skeptical" that the subprime mortgage crisis would "contaminate the whole mortgage market" and cause the economy to slip into recession. On October 1 of that year John Cochrane denied that there was a recession and predicted at worst a mild recession. In testimony before Congress in February 2008, a month before the Bear Stearns crisis, John Taylor advised against the Federal Reserve's reducing interest rates. In a speech in May, he said that interest rates were too low. He had been right years earlier when he had said they were too low, but the time when they should have been higher was long gone; to raise interest rates in a depression is disastrous.

As late as September 2008 most economists still expected a "soft landing" from the financial crisis. On September 19 Lucas expressed skepticism that the economy would slip into a recession—where it had already been for ten months. As late as September 23 Allan Meltzer opposed any government intervention, opining that the failure of Lehman Brothers had been inconsequential and that "Main Street" was doing just fine. Robert Hall was unwilling on October 10 to state that a recession had begun; one month later, Hall described the evidence that the nation was in recession as "conclusive." All these are prominent macroeconomists.

I attribute such errors of prediction not to obtuseness but to disbelief that the country could be sliding into anything worse than another of the mild recessions that we had had intermittently since the end of World War II. Many other leading macroeconomists, and prominent finance theorists as well, were simply silent as the storm gathered and broke; perhaps that was the prudent course. Even now, the profession seems adrift in uncertainty and irresolution, as if it cannot believe what has happened. No consensus has emerged with regard to how best to respond to the depression. Most economists seem willing to try virtually anything in an effort to dig the economy out of the hole into which it's fallen.

Alan Greenspan, the chairman of the Federal Reserve from 1987 to 2006, was an economist held in high regard by the economics profession. In concert with Robert Rubin and Lawrence Summers, successive Secretaries of the Treasury between 1995 and 2001, Greenspan pushed through and executed the policies that set the stage for the depression. The triumvirs refused to restrain lending, either by raising interest rates or by tightening the regulation of banks' capital structures; to bring the new financial instruments under regulation; or to prick asset-price bubbles, as the Federal Reserve could have been done (and eventually did—too late) by raising interest rates. Bernanke, a brilliant academic economist, succeeded Greenspan and continued his policies. Both missed the warning signs, and Bernanke, who became chairman of the Federal Reserve in 2006 and before then was chairman of the President's Council of Economic Advisers, was slow to accept that there would be no soft landing and that the Federal Reserve would have to trundle out its most powerful artillery to stop the slide. Had the Federal Reserve acted sooner, the bubbles would have burst with less force and the depression would probably have been averted; and likewise if it had reacted strongly when the collapse of Bear Stearns gave clear warning of a coming disaster. But I have acknowledged that there are political problems with pricking asset-price bubbles, and the Federal Reserve cannot maintain its political independence if it ruffles too many political feathers.

Not enough economists noticed (or at least remarked) the relation between executive compensation practices and risky lending, or appreciated the riskiness of mortgage-backed securities, other collateralized-debt obligations, and credit-default swaps, or connected the decline in personal savings to the danger that such lending posed to the economy. Not enough seem to have realized that the crisis of the banking industry, when it hit, was a crisis not of (or at least not mainly of) illiquidity but of insolvency. Not only were warning signs ignored until too late, but when the economics profession finally woke up we learned that neither government economists like Bernanke nor private economists had prepared any contingency plans for dealing with a depression. It should have been reasonably clear that a 20 percent or more drop in housing prices would endanger bank solvency; that such a decline in housing prices against the background of a probable housing bubble was not out of the question; and therefore that measures to strengthen the banks' balance sheets, as by increasing reserve requirements, would be prudent. Greenspan and Rubin have now apologized for their lack of foresight and preparedness, which is to their credit but does not enhance public confidence in the government's management of the economy; and lack of confidence is one of the things that cause people to hunker down in periods of economic distress by reining in their spending.

Some of the media commentary has attributed the economics profession's unsatisfactory performance to academics' being overly reliant on abstract mathematical models of the economy. But academic economists are not the only macroeconomists of note; Greenspan was not an academic before becoming chairman of the Federal Reserve. He was a consultant, and a former president of the National Association of Business Economists. And professors of finance, who are found mainly in business schools rather than in economics departments, and whose field overlaps macroeconomics in regard to recessions and depressions, tend to be deeply involved in the real world of financial markets. They are not only armchair theoreticians; they are consultants, investors, and sometimes money managers; many of them, either before joining a university faculty or during leaves of absence from the university, have worked for the Federal Reserve, the International Monetary Fund, or other nonacademic institutions. Their students typically have worked in business for several years before starting business school and so bring with them up-to-date knowledge of business practices.

The entwinement of finance professors with the financial industry has a dark side. If they criticize the industry and suggest tighter regulation, they may become black sheep and lose lucrative consultantships. This conflict of interest may have caused some economists to pull their punches. More important, few theorists spend their time poring over or digging behind banks' balance sheets. Business economists—consultants, and employees of business firms or trade associations—emphasize economic forecasting, and often have industry-specific knowledge and data, but many are compromised by their business status. One does not expect economists employed by real estate companies or by banks to be talking about housing and credit bubbles.

Insofar as the depression can be attributed to mistakes by Greenspan, Bernanke, Summers, Rubin, Paulson, and Cox (the last three not economists, however), the mistakes may be due in part to an overinvestment by economists, policymakers, and business leaders in a free-market ideology that opposes aggressive governmental interventions in the operations of the economy. Not all the economists who believe strongly in the robustness of markets and are skeptical about regulation are "conservative" across the board—economists can be liberal in the sense of being egalitarian and favoring redistributive policies without wanting to regulate corporate practices. How to make the economic pie as large as possible is a different question from whether to slice it differently. The point is only that excessive deregulation of the financial industry was a government failure abetted by the political and ideological commitments of mainstream economists, who overlooked the possibility that the financial markets seemed robust because regulation had prevented previous financial crises. The depression is a failure of capitalism, or more precisely of a certain kind of capitalism ("laissez-faire" in a loose sense, "American" versus "European" in a popular sense), and of capitalism's biggest boosters.

At the root of the profession's failure to anticipate and respond decisively to the depression is the fact that the study of depressions is a rather unsatisfactory branch of economics. Not that it is neglected by economists, the way economists nowadays neglect (for good or ill) the history of economic thought. The economic literature on depressions is voluminous and fascinating. One problem, however, is that the discontinuities (illustrated by the canoe example) that characterize depressions are hard to model. As Robert Lucas has explained, discussing the Great Depression, "How did it happen that bank failures and monetary declines translated into huge movements in employment and production? We just don't have a decent theoretical model" (quoted in *The Economics of the Great Depression*, p. 96). And who would have predicted that one reaction to an economic crisis would be a decision by a number of high-income people, widely imitated by other high-income people, to forgo conspicuous consumption that they could well afford?

Another problem with depression economics is that depressions are rare events in the life of most nations, so that to assemble a sufficiently large sample to be able to draw reliable statistical inferences that would illuminate the causes, gravity, consequences, and cures of depressions requires pooling data on depressions in different eras and different countries and thus in different, often radically different, institutional, cultural, political, and economic environments. In so heterogeneous a sample each data point is likely to be idiosyncratic. There are too many differences between America in the 1930s and Japan in the 1990s (or even between America and Japan in the 1930s, when Japan's depression was very mild compared to ours) to allow a confident inference that deficit spending, which failed to cure the Japanese depression of the 1990s, would likewise have failed to restore our prosperity even if implemented consistently during the depression of the 1930s. A further but typical complication is that while the reduction in federal government spending in 1937, coupled with a tightening of bank credit, is generally agreed to have caused the "second depression," which lasted almost until the United States entered World War II (as late as 1940 our unemployment rate was 15 percent), the effects of these simultaneous changes in policy cannot readily be distinguished. Still another complication is that the second depression may have been due in part to New Deal measures that restricted output, such as the National Industrial Recovery Act and National Labor Relations Act.

I mentioned Hitler's Germany as an example of swift recovery from the Great Depression. Heavy deficit spending on limited-access highways (the famous *Autobahnen*) and on combat aircraft, submarines, tanks, and other munitions, coupled with conscription, eliminated unemployment years before the unemployment rate in the United States dropped below 15 percent. A similar rearmament program in Japan had similar effects. Our enormous deficit spending to finance the war against the Axis corresponded to Germany's and Japan's rearmament spending—in all three cases military expenditures financed by borrowing appear to have been effective depression cures. So here are three anecdotes to support Keynes—and notice how they also support his argument that public spending can be an effective depression antidote even if it is otherwise worthless. He gave the example of hiring the unemployed to dig ditches and, having done so, to fill them up again. Military expenditures resemble the ditch-digging example (or my example of feral-cat shelters) in making no contribution to economic welfare in the usual sense. But the anecdotes provide only limited guidance for the United States in the present depression because the circumstances are so different. The power of Keynes's theory lies in its simple, commonsense logic: if the private demand for goods and services falls, so that there are unemployed productive resources, meaning resources the opportunity cost of which is by definition zero (excluding the value of leisure to the unemployed), public spending, financed by borrowing (or by money created for the occasion by the nation's central bank), can take up the slack in demand at low cost. But whether this logic is applicable to conditions in twenty-first-century America has not been established.

When competing hypotheses cannot be subjected to rigorous empirical testing, the choice between them will be heavily influenced by preconceptions. In the case of hypotheses about depressions, the preconceptions are likely in turn to be influenced by ideology, thus bringing us back to where this discussion started. Left-leaning economists tend to see depressions as evidence of the failure of unregulated capitalism and right-leaning ones to blame depressions on misguided governmental policies, without which, they believe, there would be at worst occasional mild recessions. That was Milton Friedman's view—at one time he urged the abolition of the Federal Reserve. He wanted discretionary control of the money supply by government officials to be replaced by a rule (hence the dispensability of the Fed) prescribing a constant rate of growth of the money supply. The approach may seem wacky in light of our current economic situation. But had such a rule been in force in the early 2000s the Federal Reserve could not have flooded the economy with money and by doing so set the stage for a depression. Yet there might still have been a depression (remember all the foreign capital that flowed into the United States), in which event the absence of a monetary authority with discretionary power would have been calamitous.

The ideological divisions over macroeconomic policy—divisions reflected in warring schools of macroeconomic thought, such as the monetarist, the Keynesian, the neo-Keynesian, the new classical economic, and the Austrian—preclude consensus and leave politicians and the public to wander in an untracked wilderness. The very existence of warring schools within a field is a clue that the field is weak, however brilliant its practitioners. In the current crisis, conservative economists—with the signal exception of Martin Feldstein, a chairman of the Council of Economic Advisers under President Reagan—were slow to acknowledge that the nation was even in a recession, whereas liberal economists revel in the criticisms of capitalism that a depression invites, the opportunities it provides for active government to show what it can do, and the unsound business practices and regulatory laxity that a depression brings to light and makes newsworthy. The fact that conservative economists favor a tax cut over deficit spending as a depression response reflects their hostility to big government, while the fact that liberal economists prefer public-works spending to a tax cut reflects their desire to use the depression as the launching pad for a new New Deal.

Economic understanding of the causes and cures of depressions has not progressed to the point at which ideology no longer influences analysis. When good arguments, and some evidence, are presented on both sides of an economic debate that engages the political passions that economists share with other people, but the debate cannot be resolved by empirical testing, preconceptions shaped by ideology will exert a mesmerizing influence on the debaters. Still, this depression, like the last, is likely to stimulate fresh thinking by economists, as well as to provide new data for empirical analysis. It has already stimulated a good deal of fresh thinking—on the part of Bernanke, for example. He is a conservative economist, and conservative economists don't like deficit-spending programs, or at least their public-works and transfer-payment components, which expand the government's economic footprint. Yet he supports the stimulus program, having come to doubt that a depression can be averted or cured by monetary policy alone. Many economists have been converted—virtually overnight—from being Milton Friedman monetarists to being J. M. Keynes deficit spenders, as they see monetary policy failing to deliver us from the depression. Economists are influenced by ideology, but they are not impervious to evidence. The thirteenth-century change of name of the English town of Middleton de Keynes to Milton Keynes may have been prophetic. But the speed of the profession's conversion (not that it is complete) from Friedman to Keynes suggests that the intellectual foundations of depression economics are unstable.

This discussion may help to solve another puzzle: why the press, both the financial press and the general press, was more alert to the impending crisis than economists were. Whatever their intellectual limitations relative to a Ben Bernanke or a Robert Lucas, reporters are at least not handicapped by preconceptions drawn from economic theory and economic history that seemed to have ruled out doubts about the adequacy of monetary policy for warding off depressions. They also have their noses closer to the ground than economists do, and that may enable them to sense a housing bubble or risky mortgage lending at the local level before the news reaches the Federal Reserve or the academy.

There is another difference. The press, even when it takes the sedate form of the *Economist*, thrives on drama and therefore on conflict and alarms, discord and discontinuities. Bubbles and bank insolvencies are more exciting business-news items than a rise in house prices that is driven by fundamentals, such as an increase in affluence, family size, or high prices of building materials. Reporters are primed to be alert for signs of trouble—but the other side of this coin is a tendency of experts and officials to discount their warnings as alarmist.

9

Apportioning Blame

I SAID THAT the basic responsibility for the depression rests with the private sector—with decisions such as Citigroup's to increase the amount of risk in its lending. And since we have frequent recessions, it probably is unrealistic to expect government to be able to prevent them; it prevents some and softens others and that's doubtless the best that can be expected. But given the experience of the Great Depression and the tools forged then and later to prevent a repetition, one might have expected the government to have been able to prevent a recession from molting into a depression. The measures the government took in the fall of 2008 and those it will be taking this year and next will, one hopes, prevent the current depression from sinking to the depths of the last one. But the measures taken and to be taken are very costly. They reflect the dawning belief that we really are in a depression, though the word continues to be taboo. They may do long-term damage to the economy. The global depression that our depression has sparked, moreover, contains ominous implications for world peace and for the international reputation and influence of the United States.

So the market can be blamed for recessions, which without government intervention would often turn into depressions, as they often did before the government learned (we thought!) in the aftermath of the Great Depression how to prevent that from happening. But that doesn't let the government off the hook. It failed to take timely and coherent measures to check the downturn. The seeds of failure were sown in the movement to reduce the regulation of banking and credit, which began in the 1970s. They germinated during the Clinton Administration, when the housing bubble began and the deregulation of banking culminated in the repeal of the Glass-Steagall Act (which had separated commercial banking from investment banking) and it was decided not to bring the new financial instruments, in particular credit-default swaps, under regulation even to the limited extent of moving trading in swaps to exchanges, which would have given the public information about the scope, risks, and value of these instruments. Greenspan, Rubin, and Summers, the dominant figures in U.S. economic policy during the Clinton era, allowed the head of steam to build up that would eventually blow the housing and banking industries sky-high.

But there might not have been a depression had it not been for the Bush Administration's mismanagement of the economy. Bush cannot be criticized for having reappointed Greenspan as chairman of the Federal Reserve in 2004. Greenspan had a towering reputation; it is only in hindsight that we can see that his reputation was inflated and that after seventeen years in the post he had overstayed his welcome. And Bernanke looked like a superb choice to succeed Greenspan in 2006, and probably was, though he went on to make grave mistakes. The appointment of Paulson as Secretary of the Treasury the same year was defensible, although in retrospect mistaken. But by the time Bernanke and Paulson were appointed much of the damage had been done—and they had to be given time to come up to speed in their new jobs. Paulson's predecessors as Secretary of the Treasury in the Bush Administration—Paul O'Neill and John Snow—were not financial experts. And

Bernanke was standing in the long shadow cast by Greenspan.

Bush made a mistake in firing Lawrence Lindsey, his principal economic adviser, in December 2002—primarily for his foresight in predicting, contrary to the official view, that the forthcoming war in Iraq would not be cheap (even though he greatly underestimated the expense). A Harvard Ph.D. in economics who had taught at Harvard and been a member of the Federal Reserve, Lindsey had warned in the 1990s against the dot-com bubble and would probably have been quicker than any other senior official in the Bush Administration to spot and advise action against the far more dangerous housing bubble. None of Lindsey's successors as director of the National Economic Council (the position now filled by Lawrence Summers)—Stephen Friedman, Allan Hubbard, and Keith Hennessey—was an economist and none played a visible role in economic policy. Bernanke was chairman of the Council of Economic Advisers until he became the chairman of the Federal Reserve in 2006, but he was succeeded by Edward Lazear, who although a fine economist is a labor economist rather than a macroeconomist or a financial economist. The Bush White House was not staffed to deal with a depression. This will now change. Lawrence Summers is a macroeconomist, and Lazear's successor, Christina Romer, is a specialist in depression economics.

Another mistake of the Bush Administration's management of the economy, though one the gravity of which is apparent only in hindsight, is the budget deficits of the Bush years, which so increased the size of the national debt. So great was the national debt before the financial crisis hit that the economy will be hard-pressed to absorb the enormous expenditures that are being made in an effort to spur a recovery, without doing serious long-term damage to the U.S. economy.

The budget deficits have another significance. They increased our demand for foreign capital to finance the deficits. They thus encouraged the trade policies of export-oriented countries like China, Japan, and Germany that like to collect U.S. dollars in exchange for the goods that they export to the United States and to invest the dollars here, a practice that by reducing interest rates helped set the stage for our depression (and theirs).

The divisions within the economics profession over fundamental issues of policy gave political preferences free rein to shape economic policy.

The way was open for a doctrinaire free-market, pro-business, anti-regulatory ideology to dominate the Bush Administration's economic thinking and regulatory enforcement (or nonenforcement) until the depression was upon us, whereupon ideology took a back seat. Until then the laxity of the Securities and Exchange Commission under the chairmanship of Christopher Cox was symptomatic of the Administration's economic philosophy. Little had been done to rein in risky lending by banks, and little was done to prevent a collapse of the banking system before the bailout of Bear Stearns in March 2008 and for six months afterward—until the system collapsed. It is true that when the crash came, in mid-September, the government moved with alacrity to save the major financial firms. But besides having waited too long to intervene in the deteriorating finance market, it decided to allow Lehman Brothers to slip into bankruptcy—a decision, yet to be explained, that looms as the single biggest blunder to date in the response to the gathering storm.

Lehman defaulted on some $165 billion in unsecured debt, but that was the least of the problem. It was the number-one dealer in commercial paper, a form of debt that seemed safe because of who the issuers were (large, blue-ribbon corporations) and because it was short term. The major customers for commercial paper were money market funds, which pay low interest rates because they are (or rather were) considered utterly safe. Lehman was the middleman between the issuers of commercial paper and the money market funds, and when it unexpectedly collapsed, the commercial-paper market—a significant part of the overall credit market—froze. Lehman's collapse showed that commercial paper wasn't so safe after all, so money markets stopped buying it and as a result issuers of commercial paper stopped issuing it. They had standby lines of credit at banks, however, and when all at once they tried to draw on them this further reduced the banks' ability to make new loans. One reason I have not mentioned for why the bailouts of the banking industry resulted in few new bank loans was that the banks had to use bailout money to honor previous loan commitments, which they were repeatedly called upon to do because of the credit shortage.

Lehman was also very active in the market for credit-default swaps. It had swap contracts with banks all over the world. Those banks now had to worry about how much protection they had against

Lehman's defaulting on the swaps (if they were the insured party) and how much liability to Lehman (which means, since it was now bankrupt, to its creditors) they might have if they were the insuring party. Lehman also had a strategic position in the market for letters of credit. Those are bank guaranties that a transaction will go through according to its terms, and are virtually *de rigueur* in international trade. Lehman's collapse threw a monkey wrench into international trade at a time when it was declining anyway because of the worldwide credit freeze.

The freeze on borrowing and lending in crucial markets, such as the market for commercial paper, that ensued from Lehman's sudden collapse evoked immediate steps by the government, notably the $700 billion bailout. But its implementation was delayed by the mistaken belief that the credit markets were frozen merely because of uncertainty, and not also and mainly because of the insolvency of the banks. Yet even if the government had announced the day after it let Lehman declare bankruptcy that it was going to lend $700 billion to banks to save the banking system from insolvency, it would have been too late; the damage had been done. If Lehman could go broke, any financial firm could go broke, so any such firm would be reckless if it lent a significant portion of the bailout money that it received rather than holding it in cash, or cash equivalents such as Treasury bills.

The failure to save Lehman had another consequence, which assumed growing significance in the months that followed. It shook confidence in the government's management of the crisis, as did the stumble over the $700 billion bailout and later the government's waffling about an auto bailout— first denying that any part of the $700 billion bailout fund could lawfully be used to save a nonfinancial company and then deciding, after Congress voted down an auto bailout bill, that it could give some of the bailout money to the automakers after all, without congressional authorization. This about-face undermined Bernanke's and Paulson's claim that they had lacked the legal authority to bail out Lehman. If they could lawfully bail out insolvent auto manufacturers, they could lawfully have bailed out an insolvent investment bank. It became increasingly obvious that the government had no game plan—that it was lurching from crisis to crisis in a desperate effort to arrest the decline.

Business requires a reasonably stable political environment. Because the bailout program was completely ad hoc, banks did not know where they stood. Private recapitalization of the banks was made impossible by uncertainty. Who in his right mind would invest in a bank without knowing what the government would do if the bank got into trouble? What banker would be fool enough to lend the capital his bank received from the government without knowing whether the government would give the bank more capital when borrowers defaulted on their loans? Never having dreamed that it might be necessary to recapitalize the banking industry, the Federal Reserve and the Treasury Department had no plan for recapitalization—which meant among other things that when Paulson and his staff departed on January 20, the incoming Treasury officials had no plan to work from. The cries that the administration of the bailout plan lacked "transparency" and "accountability" (perhaps this will now change) are correct. But the simpler and more important point is that the banks have no idea what is going to happen to them, and this reinforces their natural reluctance (because they are undercapitalized) to lend and their inability to attract private capital. The prospect of a regulatory overhaul can only deepen the banks' uncertainty and increase their paralysis.

Had there been contingency plans for dealing with a depression, the politicization of the response, of which conservatives complain with particular reference to the stimulus package and liberals with particular reference to the bailouts, would have been less. There would have been apolitical plans drawn up by professionals, and the burden would have been shifted to the politicians to defy professional counsel in pursuit of what would be exposed as nakedly political ends.

It did not help that President Bush gave the impression of lacking interest in or engagement with the growing crisis. No one expects a President to be a financial expert. (Mitt Romney would have been the first.) No one expects him to be a military expert either, but he is expected to exercise overall direction of a war, and likewise with a struggle to prevent a depression. The American and world publics would have expected the President of the United States to focus all his energies on the financial crisis, to master the basics, and to address the nation and the world in a confident and reassuring tone, not belittling the difficulties but explaining them in simple yet not condescending terms and conveying a sense of competent and determined leadership. Instead he (and, so far as appeared to the outside world at any rate, his Domestic Economic Council and Council of Economic Advisers) abdicated to Bernanke and Paulson, neither of whom is a politician and neither of whom has the communications skills that the emergency required. But at least Bush didn't allow orthodox conservative thinking to block pragmatic responses by Bernanke and Paulson, without which the financial crisis would be even worse than it is.

Uncertainty about what Bernanke and Paulson were going to do next was compounded by uncertainty about what the new Administration would do come January 20, 2009, which was soon further compounded by uncertainty about what a surprisingly assertive Democratic-controlled Congress would let the new Administration do. These uncertainties, combined with doubts about the competence of the government's economic management, created an impossible environment for business planning. Congress is less to blame for having pushed in previous years for risky mortgage loans to promote homeownership—for it was pushing against an open door—than for the squabbling and grandstanding and demagoguery and delay that have been its principal contributions to date to rescuing the economy. Congress is operating without an economic gyroscope. Most of its members do not understand the economic crisis and wish to use it as an occasion for scoring political points and advancing political agendas unrelated to the needs of the moment. This is shown by their eagerness to promote unionization in a depression.

The successive Federal Reserve chairmanships of Greenspan and Bernanke must be reckoned prime causes of the financial crisis and the slide into depression. Greenspan's tremendous prestige gave him a largely free hand, which he did not use, to choke off the housing bubble by raising interest rates and to rein in risky lending by exercising more assertively the control that the Federal Reserve has over commercial banks. He thought he could avoid political controversy by waiting for bubbles to form and pop and cleaning up afterward by lowering interest rates. He was the prisoner of past successes— the strategy had worked when Long-Term Capital Management collapsed in 1998, when the dot-com bubble burst in 2000, and when the stock market dipped as a result of the 9/11 attacks. But each flood of money into the economy set the stage for the next bubble, while at the same time lulling the business community into believing that the Federal Reserve would always assure a soft landing from a burst bubble by a timely reduction in interest rates. Apparently Bernanke thought similarly: any fallout from the bursting of the housing bubble or from the near collapse of Countrywide in 2007 or the collapse of Bear Stearns the following spring could be neutralized by lowering interest rates.

The Duke of Wellington remarked that a great victory is a great danger. Success breeds complacence. Or as William Blake said, damn braces—bless relaxes. Greenspan's triumphs and laurels ill prepared him and his successor to confront a new crisis with fresh thinking.

A further point is that ever since the "stagflation" of the 1970s—the mysterious-seeming confluence of high inflation with low economic growth—the preoccupation of business-cycle macroeconomists had been with preventing inflation by keeping interest rates up but not so far up as to precipitate a recession. Greenspan seemed in the early 2000s to have squared the circle—interest rates were kept down but inflation, though it did increase, stayed within tolerable limits. Actually what seems to have been happening is that cheap imports from China and elsewhere, along with a healthy growth in productivity, kept prices of most goods and services low and diverted the inflationary pressure created by Greenspan's monetary policy into asset prices that did not have a substantial influence on the consumer price index, notably the price of houses. Because real estate is heavily financed by debt, when debt is cheap the demand for real estate grows. Because houses are extremely durable goods, the stock of housing grows only slowly; and when the supply of a good is inelastic, an increase in demand can cause a large increase in price because supply cannot quickly be increased to the level of the new demand.

When it seemed that we could have low interest rates without unacceptable inflation, worries about recession receded, since low interest rates encourage economic activity and thus reduce the danger of recession. It is when low interest rates create inflation that a threat of recession looms, because the Federal Reserve will be motivated to raise interest rates in order to break the inflation; that was the cause of the severe 1980–1982 recession. That low interest rates might cause a credit binge that would cause a recession and even a depression was off the policy radar screen, in part because the synergistic effect of cheap credit and financial deregulation was missed. It was like winning World War II and being blindsided by guerrilla warfare in Vietnam.

The United States had had plenty of experience with such warfare in earlier days, notably in the Philippines, but that seemed ancient history, as did the Great Depression—until a few months ago.

So there is blame aplenty to go around and there are also the adventitious factors that I mentioned earlier—the timing of the crisis in relation to the presidential campaign and transition and the Christmas shopping season. So there were failures of the free market, failures of economic science, failures of government—and some bad luck into the bargain.

Some readers may think that I am being too critical of the Federal Reserve and the economics profession and have let the financiers off too lightly—which may seem inconsistent with my claim that this depression is a failure of capitalism. But although the financiers bear the primary *responsibility* for the depression, I do not think they can be *blamed* for it—implying moral censure—any more than one can blame a lion for eating a zebra. Capitalism is Darwinian. Businessmen take risks (mostly within the law) that promote their financial interest; it would make no more sense for an individual businessman to worry that because of the instability of the banking industry his decisions and those of his competitors might trigger a depression than for a lion to spare a zebra out of concern that lions are eating zebras faster than the zebras can reproduce. To tell banks not to make risky loans— to upbraid them for "an unquenchable thirst for easy profits" or for taking "unjustifiable risks for their own gain, and in so doing jeopardiz[ing] the future of the nation's credit system and now the economy itself" (in the overheated words of the economic journalist Jeff Madrick)—or to upbraid a homebuyer for taking out a mortgage loan that he may be unable to repay, is like telling lions and zebras to build a fence between them.

The journalists and politicians, and some who should know better, like the distinguished macroeconomist Paul Krugman, are engaged in an orgy of recrimination against Wall Street. They have the wrong target. The responsibility for building the fences that prevent an economic collapse as a result of risky lending devolves on the government. It is true that politics is Darwinian in much the same sense as capitalism is; politicians compete for votes, corresponding to dollars. But the Federal Reserve, like the federal courts, has considerable though not complete insulation from politics. For thirty years the chairmen of the Federal Reserve have been economists attentive to academic thinking about the proper role of the Fed. The two most recent chairmen, Greenspan and Bernanke, made serious economic mistakes. But it is not their economic mistakes that are culpable; those mistakes were so widely shared by other experts in macroeconomics and finance theory that they cannot be regarded as individual failures. Nor can economics be blamed for economists' imperfect understanding of the causes and cures of depressions, any more than chemistry can be blamed for not having achieved a complete understanding of crystallization. Every science has an agenda of unsolved problems. What Bernanke and Greenspan and the academy can be blamed for is overconfidence in their understanding of how to prevent a depression and, as a result, a failure to attend to warning signs and a lack of preparedness.

Robert Lucas, than whom no living macro-economist is more distinguished, said in his presidential address to the American Economic Association in January 2003: "Macroeconomics was born as a distinct field in the 1940s, as a part of the intellectual response to the Great Depression. The term then referred to the body of knowledge and expertise that we hoped would prevent the recurrence of that economic disaster. My thesis in this lecture is that macroeconomics in this original sense has succeeded: *Its central problem of depression-prevention has been solved, for all practical purposes, and has in fact been solved for many decades*" (emphasis added). I don't think he would say that today.

It was well known that asset-price bubbles can endanger a nation's banking industry and that if the banking industry fails the nation can be plunged into a 1930s-style depression, and as early as 2003 there were warnings from reputable sources that a bubble was building in the housing industry. For want of advance planning, the housing bubble was allowed to develop and expand until it burst, a credit bubble was allowed to develop and expand until *it* burst, and the response to the crash when it came in September 2008 consisted of a series of desperate improvisations that deepened the crisis by conveying to business and the general public an impression of fear, bluff, and indecision.

10

The Way Forward

BAILOUTS, EASY MONEY, stimulus, a moratorium on foreclosures, and any other emergency measures taken to limit the length and severity of a depression are just damage control. And expensive damage control. The cures for depression are not worse than the sickness, but they are bad enough. We need to begin thinking about ways of reducing the probability of another depression; most important we need to insist on the formulation of the contingency plans that the Federal Reserve and the Treasury Department so tragically failed to formulate. We cannot just say, well, the last depression was three quarters of a century ago so we don't need to start worrying about heading off the next one until, say, 2080. That would not be prudent, not only because everything happens faster nowadays but also because low-probability events can occur at any time. The forces that led to the present depression do not have a memory to tell them to wait eighty years (1929–2009) before foregathering again.

There were three big prevention failures this time: excessive deregulation, neglect of warning signs, and insouciance about the decline in the rate of personal savings and the safety of such savings. These are corrigible, at least to a degree. The first two are related. The existence of multiple federal financial regulatory bodies — including the Federal Reserve, the Federal Deposit Insurance Corporation, the Securities Investor Protection Corporation, the Securities and Exchange Commission, the Commodity Futures Trading Commission, the Federal Housing Administration, the Federal Housing and Finance Administration, the Office of Housing Enterprise Oversight, the National Credit Union Administration, the Treasury Department and its agencies, such as the Comptroller of the Currency and the Office of Thrift Supervision — and fifty state banking and insurance commissioners — has led to a fragmentation of regulatory authority, a lack of coordination, turf wars, yawning regulatory gaps with respect to hedge funds, bank substitutes, and novel financial instruments, and an inability to aggregate and analyze information about emerging problems in the financial markets.

Banks often are able by small changes in form to choose which agency to be regulated by. Consolidation of the regulatory agencies (as in Germany and the United Kingdom—and a partial consolidation was proposed by our Treasury Department in March 2008) would improve the government's ability to regulate financial markets effectively and to spot financial crises in their incipience. An international financial regulatory authority may be necessary as well, given the interdependence of the banking systems of the different nations.

And because safe personal savings (and not just overpriced common stocks and overmortgaged houses) are an important check against depressions, and heavy personal borrowing is a risk factor for them, consideration should perhaps be given to placing limits on credit card and mortgage credit, on easy credit generally, and on the right (which fosters overindebtedness) to eliminate debts by declaring bankruptcy. Other regulatory changes might be desirable, such as limiting leverage, raising credit-rating standards and changing how credit-rating agencies are compensated, forbidding proprietary trading by banks (that is, trading of their equity capital, which puts that capital at risk), adjusting reserve requirements to take more realistic account of the riskiness of banks' capital structures, requiring greater disclosure by hedge funds and private equity funds, requiring that credit-default swaps be traded on exchanges and fully collateralized, and even resurrecting usury laws. Obviously this is just a partial list.

But this is not the time either to reorganize or to reregulate the financial industry. The case against reorganization is the clearer: experience, as with the Department of Homeland Security, teaches that a major federal reorganization (not to mention a reorganization that would encompass both state and foreign regulation of financial intermediation as well) takes years to gel, and during those years of growing pains the efficiency with which the mission entrusted to the reorganized entity will be performed will be lower than it was in the pre-reorganization regime. And this is apart from the fact that in the present instance the same small knot of senior economic officials that would design and supervise the reorganization have their hands full dealing with an economic emergency.

The case against trying to reregulate financial intermediation at this time is a bit subtler and requires me to distinguish between two senses of "regulation." In one sense it refers to the regulatory *framework*—the laws that establish the powers and limits of the regulatory body. In another sense it refers to the regulatory *regime*—the actual administration of the regulatory scheme, which involves the exercise by officials of discretion within the limits set by the legal framework. "Deregulation" usually refers to changing the regulatory framework in the direction of relaxing controls over the regulated firms in order to make the market freer and more competitive. In that sense the deregulation movement in the financial industry was largely completed in the 1990s. But because deregulation of the regulatory framework is usually and in this instance incomplete, "deregulation" can also refer to changes in the regulatory regime, and in that sense deregulation continued making long strides, which turned out to be missteps, in the 2000s. Alan Greenspan, exercising the vast discretion reposed by Congress in the Federal Reserve, decided to push interest rates down and keep them down. He and his successor also decided to use a light touch in regulating banking practices, over which the Federal Reserve also has vast discretionary control. Notably the Fed can increase a bank's reserve requirements (and thus constrain its ability to lend) if it determines that the bank's capital is too risky. The Bush Administration took a decidedly hands-off attitude toward the financial sector, typified by the passivity of the Securities and Exchange Commission under Cox's chairmanship. A regime of laxity inhabited a rickety framework.

All this will now change, just as the civil rights regime of the Clinton Administration, which emphasized race and gender discrimination, gave way to the Bush Administration's civil rights regime, which emphasized religious discrimination. But until the new, bound-to-be activist regulatory regime (in which Bernanke, though a holdover, is likely to participate willingly) has had a chance to show what it can do within the existing regulatory framework, it is premature to alter the framework.

And for the further reason that while re-regulation is likely to be administratively less complex than reorganization (just count the federal and state agencies that would have to be included in one way or another in the reorganization for it to be maximally effective), it is more challenging intellectually. There is first the extraordinary diversity and complexity of modern financial intermediation. Commercial banks conduct little more than half the financial intermediation in the American economy. If they are forced to be safe, their competitors will eat them alive. But can hedge funds, private equity funds, investment banks, and all the other nonbank banks be placed under the identical regulatory regime as commercial banks? If not, won't the differences distort competition?

It is easier to deregulate an industry than to re-regulate it. Deregulation has a built-in momentum: allow an unregulated firm to compete with a regulated one and the regulated firm will have a convincing case that it must be deregulated so that it can compete. One ends with a competitive industry. The competitive financial-intermediation industry that deregulation has created is complex and varied. The industry cannot readily be made homogeneous, yet its heterogeneity greatly magnifies the difficulty of designing and implementing a comprehensive system of regulation.

We could, in principle anyway, restore the regulatory framework of commercial banking that existed in the 1960s. Bank capital would consist mainly of zero-interest demand deposits and federal securities and would be used mainly to make short-term commercial loans. But we know that this model of banking would not be viable if other financial intermediaries were permitted, as they are today, to offer close substitutes for bank products. Does this mean, however, that money market funds, hedge funds, and all the other nonbank banks must be placed under the same regulatory controls as commercial banks? Should they for example be required to have reserves? To pay zero interest to the lenders of their capital? If the answer to these questions is yes, that is the end of hedge funds, of money market funds, etc. If the answer is no, it is unclear how much reregulation of commercial banks is possible. If there is another answer, it will take much thought to work out.

There is a further and very serious complication. As far as I know, no one has a clear sense of the social value of our deregulated financial industry, with its free-wheeling banks and hedge funds and private equity funds and all the rest. The profits were, until the financial crisis of last fall, enormous, but undoubtedly contained a large amount of economic rent. (This is related to the point I made in chapter 6 about the possible overcompensation of physics Ph.D.'s who go to work for Wall Street.) When A sells B stock worth $10 a share, and the next day it is worth $15, the country is not

$5 richer, though B is. Obviously a stock exchange and a credit system are enormous public goods (as we are learning anew in this depression), but the value added by the vast increases in recent years in the amount of speculative trading is unclear. Until we get a clear idea of what it is, we do not know what the costs would be of adopting a 1960s-style model of the financial system, or, more realistically, taking some large steps in that direction. Reregulation, like reorganization, should wait.

Short of comprehensive reregulation, a few piecemeal reforms may be feasible and helpful. But I am afraid that the list that follows is pretty small beer. Maybe, for example, the government should stop talking up homeownership. True, there is an argument and some evidence that homeownership creates external benefits because owners care more about the appearance of their house and their neighborhood than an absentee landlord does, and the entire neighborhood benefits. But since most owned homes as distinct from rented ones are detached houses located in suburbs, homeownership promotes suburban sprawl, traffic congestion, and carbon emissions. The exemption from federal income tax of interest on residential mortgages (including home equity loans) and of real estate taxes is a heavy subsidy for homeownership. It is subsidy enough, or more than enough. There is no good argument for the government's propagandizing for homeownership and pushing banks to make risky mortgage loans.

I mentioned that among the bubble factors were the level and structure of executive compensation. Efforts to place legal limits on compensation are bound to fail, or to be defeated by loopholes, or to cause distortions in the executive labor market and in corporate behavior. An example would be limiting bonuses to financial executives. The fact that the banking industry paid billions of dollars in bonuses in 2008 is arousing the ignorant indignation of the press and the calculated indignation of politicians. As much as half the income of such executives consists of bonuses, and this enables a better matching of income to performance than flat salaries do. So to have eliminated all bonuses would have amounted to a 50 percent salary cut for many financial executives. The bonuses were smaller than in previous years, so there was a salary cut, and that was appropriate; it is unclear whether a greater cut would have been optimal.

Measures short of capping compensation may be worth considering, though I cannot work up a great deal of enthusiasm for them. Initially, at least, they should be limited to executives of banks and other financial intermediaries, as that is where executive-compensation practices menace the entire economy. The effect would be to drive some financial executives (and prospective financial executives) into other fields, but that would not be a bad thing, as I have explained. The biggest problem is that to be effective in reducing the likelihood of catastrophic bank failures, the limits on compensation could not be confined to CEOs and other senior officials. The actual trading decisions are made lower down in the corporate hierarchy. It is hard to see how the government could fix a salary schedule for the entire professional staff of a bank.

A simple, and I imagine an inevitable, reform would be to require corporations, both those that are publicly held (that is, their stock is traded on an exchange and the ownership of the stock is widely dispersed) and those that are privately held (otherwise the requirement will drive many publicly held firms private), to disclose the *full* compensation of all senior executives. This would include pension entitlements discounted to present value, health benefits, severance pay, private use of corporate facilities including airplanes, limousines, and apartments, club memberships paid for by the corporation, and all other perquisites, monetized where possible and subject to public audit.

A second fairly modest reform would be to require that a substantial share of the compensation of financial executives be backloaded and tied to the corporation's future performance. For example, a corporation might be forbidden to provide severance pay to its CEO (though it could pay him a signing bonus, since that wouldn't give him an incentive to impart greater risk to the corporation) and required to pay him a specified percentage of his compensation in the form of restricted stock in the corporation—stock that he could not sell (or redeem, in the case of a privately held corporation) for a specified number of years. Such a reform would combat the dangerous incentive of highly compensated CEOs to maximize short-term corporate profits and, to that end, to take excessive risks with the corporation's assets.

The problem (it is the same as the problem of stock options) is that the performance of an individual employee in a large corporation, even if he is the CEO, is unlikely to have a measurable effect on the value of the corporation's stock. An alternative that is receiving increasing attention, probably rightly so, is "claw back": part of the employee's bonus is placed in an account, and if he has a bad year the account is reduced. This is an effective method of fitting pay to performance if the employee is solely or primarily responsible for specific transactions involving measurable profits or losses.

Consideration should perhaps be given to increasing the marginal income tax rate of persons who have very high incomes, in order to reduce their appetite for risk-taking. Such incomes typically contain a good deal of economic rent. Think of the boxing champion who makes millions but whose next best job would be as a bouncer in a strip joint, paid the minimum wage. Taxing economic rents is efficient because it has, by definition (and in my example), minimal substitution effects. It will not deflect the taxpayer to a different occupation just because it taxes the income available to him only in his present one. An increase in income tax cannot very well be limited to financial executives—it would be like making them wear dunce caps—but I do not think there is a compelling objection to raising the marginal tax rate on *all* high earners. Taxes will have to be raised at some point in order to finance the anti-depression programs, and income taxes are more efficient taxes than, say, corporate taxes. The refusal or inability of the Bush Administration either to raise taxes or to reduce spending caused a dangerous increase in the national debt. This is not the time to raise taxes, but we are an undertaxed nation.

The suggested measures have drawbacks. For example, in practice progressive taxation abounds with loopholes and distorts the allocation of resources, and unless it took the form of an excess-profits tax, which would be unmanageable, it would hit indiscriminately incomes that did and incomes that did not contain substantial economic rents. And forcing greater transparency on financial corporations by requiring them to disclose publicly the full value of their senior executives' compensation might turn out to be a case of closing the barn door after the horses have escaped. For in the wake of the financial crisis the debate over CEO compensation has become so heated that efforts to conceal such compensation are likely to fail. Maybe the attainment of transparency can be left to the market, aided by aggressive financial media.

About all that can be said for the measures that I have suggested may warrant consideration now, while the depression is ongoing, is that they skirt the profound and intractable issues involved in deciding whether to reregulate financial intermediation.

A further point may be worth noting. The existing regulatory protections of investors and consumers, including corporate-governance regulations designed to align executives' incentives with overall economic welfare, and the existing regulation of mortgages and other forms of credit, should not be thought of as merely investor-protection or consumer-protection measures, akin to laws against fraud. They are also macroeconomic tools, like the Federal Reserve's power to raise interest rates—a power that failed to prevent the crisis of 2008.

But the point I particularly wish to emphasize is that the President and his advisers have their hands full dealing with the depression and with a series of urgent foreign and security policy issues. It is a temptation, but would I think be a mistake, for the new Administration to try to emulate Franklin Roosevelt's astonishing first hundred days. The United States fortunately is in less desperate straits today and American government and the American economy, and specifically the American banking system, are all immensely more complex than they were in 1933. It would take years for a new system of financial regulation administered by a newly consolidated regulatory administration to shake down. The six or eight government responses to the depression that are or soon will be under way are enough for now. Let the comprehensive structural solution await calmer days.

II

The Future of Conservatism

THE DEFEAT of the Republican Party in the November 2008 election—a defeat the magnitude of which probably owed a lot to the financial crisis and the inept response to it of the McCain campaign—is widely thought to have marked the eclipse of conservatism in the United States. The Bush Administration's indecisive response to the gathering depression in its last few months in power invites comparison to Hoover's ineffectual efforts in his lame-duck phase to check the deepening depression. Hoover's failure ushered in twenty years of Democratic Party dominance. The Bush Administration's response to the crisis, although belated, was far more vigorous than Hoover's (and Hoover had almost three and a half years to respond to his economic crisis). But it will get little credit for that because of the impression that President Bush gave, rightly or wrongly, of being AWOL while the economy was melting beneath his feet. And his Administration's responses to the crisis were inept, despite all that had been learned since Hoover's time about depressions — but perhaps not that much had been learned!

We should distinguish between the Republican Party and conservatism. Political parties in a two-party system are opportunistic coalitions and as a result lack ideological homogeneity, especially in a culturally heterogeneous nation such as the United States. Apart from the many Republicans and Democrats who vote for a party out of habit, nostalgia, or family tradition, or out of attachment to a particular issue — or even out of a personal liking or loathing for the other people who vote for a party — there are ideological voters. In the Republican Party they fall into three main groups: believers in (1) free markets, low taxes, and small government — economic conservatives; (2) believers in tough criminal laws and a strong foreign policy — I'll call them security conservatives; and (3) social (mainly religious) conservatives, who are hostile to abortion, gay marriage, pornography, gun control, and a clean separation of church and state. The security and social conservatives converge on hostility to illegal immigrants. The economic and security conservatives are in some tension because a national-security state requires a big government and therefore high taxes, and the economic conservatives are in tension with the social conservatives because the former are libertarian and the latter are interventionist.

All three groups have been damaged by recent events and are moving apart from each other because of the blows that the others have received. The depression has hit economic libertarians in their solar plexus, because it is largely a consequence not of the government's overregulating the economy and by doing so fettering free enterprise, but rather of innate limitations of the free market— limitations rooted in individuals' incentives, in irresponsible monetary policy adopted and executed by conservative officials inspired by conservative economists who thought that easy money was no problem if it did not lead to serious inflation, and in excessive, ideologically motivated deregulation of banking and finance compounded by lax enforcement of the remaining regulations. The depression and the Bush Administration's unsteady response to it, in combination with its lavish predepression deficit spending, have greatly damaged the Republicans' reputation for fiscal rectitude.

Believers in a strong foreign policy have been embarrassed by the protracted, expensive, and distracting war in Iraq—a war that has sown discord between the United States and its allies, increased recruitment of Islamic terrorists, strengthened Iran, and strengthened the Taliban and Al-Qaeda in Afghanistan and Pakistan. Security conservatives have also been embarrassed by the Bush Administration's lack of success in meeting challenges to U.S. security posed by Iran, North Korea, Afghanistan, Pakistan, and the Arab-Israeli conflict. Social conservatives have been damaged by the stridency of some of their most prominent advocates, who sometimes give the impression of being mean-spirited, out-of-touch, know-nothing deniers of science—notably of evolution, manmade climate change, sexual orientation, and even brain death (the Terri Schiavo affair).

These wounds, along with a sense of the Bush Administration's lack of managerial competence, have weakened Republican claims to be dependable trustees of the economy, of the national security, and of the moral life of the nation. The efficiency gap between the competing presidential campaigns reinforced the appearance of a competence gap between the parties. During the campaign, with McCain as well as Bush seeming incapable of understanding the economic crisis, a number of conservatives switched their support to Obama. Thoughtful conservatives, already disturbed by the cascade of blunders by the Bush Administration, culminating in its hesitant and erratic response to the financial crisis that it had failed to anticipate yet had done much to nurture by its regulatory laxity, were appalled at the intellectual vacuity of the Republican presidential campaign, its economic populism, and its preoccupation with abortion and guns as political issues of transcendent national importance.

The Republican Party flaunted the anti-intellectualism of its supporters, deriding highly educated people who speak in complete sentences as "elitists"—an attitude that sorted badly with the strong intellectual tradition of conservatism. It is a self-defeating strategy of conservatives to argue that all intellectuals are liberal and therefore conservatives should think with their guts rather than their brains. The economic crisis in which the nation finds itself cannot be solved in the gut.

This is not to paper over the failures of liberalism. The nation has accumulated a substantial history of both liberal and conservative failures. The liberal failures include lack of realism about human nature, nostalgia for failed social experiments such as adversarial unionization, underestimation of the social costs of egalitarian nostrums and of social engineering by judges (the Warren Court, *Roe v. Wade*, the near abolition of capital punishment), and underestimation of the social benefits of discipline, of punishment, of enforcing principles of personal responsibility, and of military force. The conservative failures include a nostalgia for the social values of the 1950s or earlier, a strong tendency to deny inconvenient facts (such as the human contribution to global warming), and an overestimation of the efficiency of unregulated markets, the efficacy of military force, and the beneficent effects of religiosity in public life. Liberals are wrong to promote adversarial unionism and conservatives are wrong to discourage sex education in public schools and promote abstinence as a substitute for condoms in preventing teenage pregnancy. Liberals are trapped in fantasies of equality and conservatives in the dogma of economic libertarianism and often in religious dogmas as well. At present the conservative failures stand out more because the nation has just come to the end of an unpopular Republican administration—unpopular, as I have noted, even among many conservatives—and because those failures have been highlighted in a most dramatic way by the depression that the nation now finds itself in.

I know it isn't *really* possible to think without preconceptions—I made the point earlier. As Bayesian decision theory teaches, a rational decision-maker starts with a prior probability of some uncertain event (that a credit crunch will turn into a depression, for example) but adjusts that probability as new evidence comes to his attention. Yet this means that his prior belief—his preconception—may, depending on the strength and direction of the evidence, affect his ultimate decision. That decision will be based on his posterior probability that the event will occur—the probability that he arrives at by updating his prior probability by whatever evidence he can find that bears on the matter. Nor do I mean to deny the value of theory, in particular economic theory, in guiding policy; economics has provided the framework of my analysis in this book. But there is a difference between rational preconceptions, based on theory and experience, and rigid emotional preconceptions, such as dogmatic libertarianism or egalitarianism or ungrounded hopeful beliefs such as that everybody in the world is yearning for democracy and all democrats are friends of America. Such preconceptions, which can seize a decision-maker's mind when disagreement among the experts deprives him of authoritative guidance, tell one more about the thinker's personality and the limitations of his experience and imagination than about his competence to make sensible decisions, and may be impervious to reconsideration in the light of new evidence.

The spectrum of respectable macroeconomic theorizing runs from left interventionists to right libertarians. It would be a mistake to commit to either extreme, because neither can yet be shown to be correct. The interventionists are prone to underestimate the virtues of markets and the libertarians to exaggerate them. The latter tendency is more dangerous at the present juncture. Libertarian economists failed to grasp the dangers of deregulating the financial markets and underestimated the risk and depth of the financial crisis. Their influence was a factor in the government's allowing a self-inflicted capitalist wound to infect the economy with its first depression in three quarters of a century.

The solution is not to banish politics from economic policymaking. Although in principle policies dedicated to economic efficiency would make everyone better off if supplemented by transfers from the people who benefit the most from economic growth to those who benefit the least or not at all, no one imagines that such transfers would be feasible. There are conflicts within society that can be resolved only by political competition. Only politics can adjudicate and mitigate the inevitable conflicts between groups that have different values and interests. And it is not as if turning governance over to a cadre of technical experts is a surefire solution to economic or any other problems of government. Brilliant people screw up all the time.

The space for pragmatic, apolitical, nonideological solutions to economic crises can be enlarged. A hopeful note has been sounded by the Obama Administration's decision to follow monetarist *and* deficit-spending prescriptions for curing a depression. Since no one knows which is better, and since the economic situation appears to be extremely grave, the prudent course is to try both without worrying which is the more liberal or the more conservative. We recall that there are three rival deficit-spending approaches and two monetarist approaches, plus bailouts. Six social experiments (at least) will be going on at the same time, rather than having one approach be adopted on theoretical grounds at the outset.

It is true that by taking several approaches simultaneously, the government may make it impossible to determine the value of each approach, just as in 1937, when the government both raised interest rates (an anti-monetarist measure, because raising interest rates reduces the money supply) and curtailed public spending (an anti-Keynesian measure, because public spending is the Keynesian recipe for ending a depression). By taking these measures the government prolonged the depression—and no one can be sure which measure had the worse effect. At the end of the present depression, the theoretical, ideologically salted struggle between monetarists and deficit spenders will resume if it turns out to be impossible to separate the effects of the different measures.

Until then, let us hope that economists respond to the crisis in the spirit of pragmatism rather than of ideology. They may not agree on the best way to cure or at least shorten a depression, but they can provide decision-makers with the range of plausible policies, the spectrum of responsible professional opinion, the pros and cons of alternative measures, and, not least, an awareness of the limits of economic understanding.

Conclusion

THIS IS NOT a long book, but it has covered a lot of ground, and a brief recapitulation may be helpful.

We are in a depression. (Some economists will not acknowledge a depression until they see bread-lines and Hoovervilles.) It is the product of a financial crisis that resulted from the confluence of two dangerous developments: low interest rates in the early 2000s and the deregulation movement, which began in the 1970s. Low interest rates make borrowing cheap and make safe saving (as by purchasing certificates of deposit or other very safe interest-bearing securities) unattractive, so personal debt rises and the personal savings rate declines. Because houses are bought mainly with debt (a long-term mortgage), low interest rates encourage the purchase of houses, and because the stock of housing expands only slowly, an increase in the demand for houses leads to an increase in their prices. Low interest rates, by stimulating economic activity (people borrow to spend), tend to increase stock values, so people tend to buy common stock in lieu of safe securities. Thus, with low interest rates, people's savings increasingly take the form of pricey houses and pricey stocks—and rising prices convince people that houses and stocks are good investments.

The demand for credit is met primarily by financial intermediaries, that is, by companies—classically, commercial banks—that borrow from one group of firms or individuals and turn around and lend the borrowed money to another group. To make a profit the intermediary must pay a lower interest rate for his borrowed capital than he charges for his loans. As a practical matter this requires him to offer safety to the persons he borrows from and to assume risk in the loans he makes. This is typically done by borrowing short and lending long. A person will charge a low interest rate if he can quickly get back the money he has lent, because there is less risk of losing it and it gives him greater liquidity (the ability to put one's hands on cash when needed). He will charge a higher interest rate for a long-term loan because it will not be liquid and because something untoward that might cause the borrower to default is likelier to occur over a long period of time than over a short one. Banking thus is inherently risky; if a bank experiences a lot of defaults on its loans, its creditors—the persons who have provided it with short-term capital—will become anxious and yank their money.

The inherent riskiness of banking, and the importance of credit in a commercial society, led to strict regulation of banking, producing a system in which banks' principal capital consisted of demand deposits that banks were forbidden to pay interest on. With this cheap source of capital, banks could make a profit by making short-term rather than long-term loans, and thus were not at high risk of loss in their loan portfolios. Federal deposit insurance capped safe banking by making depositors unworried about such losses.

The deregulation movement that began in the 1970s was aimed at the regulated industries in general, and encompassed banking only because it was highly regulated. The economists and eventually the politicians who pressed for deregulation were not sensitive to the fact that deregulating banking has a macroeconomic significance that deregulating railroads or trucking or airlines or telecommunications or oil pipelines does not. The deregulation of banking proceeded along two paths. Financial intermediaries that were not banks, such as investment banks, money market funds, and hedge funds, were increasingly permitted to offer close substitutes for conventional bank services. An example is a checkable interest-bearing account in a money market fund—a close substitute for a checking account in a bank, not quite as safe but quite safe and paying interest, which checkable bank accounts in a bank did not. The second path was relaxing the regulatory restrictions on banks to enable them to compete with the nonbank financial intermediaries that were crowding them. Increasingly banks relied on short-term credit other than deposits, and increasingly they lent long as well as short; their lending thus was increasingly risky.

With the low interest rates of the early 2000s, the banks and other financial intermediaries found it convenient and profitable to meet the huge demand for loans for the purchase of housing (and also for the purchase of commercial real estate, automobiles, and items bought with credit cards, and for college tuition) by borrowing, and by borrowing more rather than by raising equity capital, thus increasing the ratio of debt to equity in their capital structure (that is, increasing their leverage). Deregulation had made the banking industry (broadly defined, as it should be, to include the other financial intermediaries, as they were more and more like banks) more competitive, squeezing profit margins. High leverage enabled small profit margins to become large ones—as long as the rate of default on the banks' loans was low. Leverage magnifies profits, but equally losses, because debts are a fixed obligation, due and owing regardless of how profitable or unprofitable the banks' lending and other investing turn out to be.

The trends toward easy credit and deregulated and therefore risky lending were mutually reinforcing. Banks realized this and tried to reduce the riskiness of their loan portfolios without reducing profit by devices such as securitized debt (notably securities backed by residential mortgages) and credit-default swaps (insurance against defaults), which dispersed risk and therefore reduced the risks borne by a particular bank. These instruments did reduce risk, but also increased it, making the net effect on the banking industry's risk unclear; for example, banks both issued and bought credit-default swaps—they were insurers of defaults as well as being insured against them. The riskiness of securitized debt was hard to assess because of the complexity of the securities, a single one of which might be backed by hundreds or even thousands of mortgages on houses scattered all over the country. Elaborate mathematical models ("value of risk" models) were created to enable banks to try to quantify the risks that their increasingly complex and risky capital structures and business practices had created.

It is widely believed that the able and often brilliant executives of the major banks and other financial intermediaries, many of which had long histories of outstanding success (such as Goldman Sachs), were actually stupid, and that that is why the banking system collapsed in September 2008. I do not agree. I do not believe that the financial crisis is the result of stupidity or irrationality, criminality or even ignorance. I think that even most of the consumers who bought houses with mortgages they could not "afford" knew what they were doing—speculating not unreasonably on a continued rise in house prices; for had not Bernanke himself declared in October 2005, shortly before the housing bubble burst, that those high prices were *not* a bubble phenomenon? The banks knew they were taking a lot of risks, and that if they faced a cascade of defaults they could go broke. Hence the efforts at diversification and the risk-management models. The banks knew that because they were heavily invested in the housing industry, if housing prices fell steeply there would be many defaults. They also knew that they (and therefore other financial intermediaries as well) were entangled with each other—a bank might originate a mortgage-backed security and sell a piece of it to another bank and at the same time buy a piece of a similar security issued by that other bank.

Though I am not certain of this, I believe that the senior executives of the major banks were aware that there might be at least a small probability of bankruptcy as a result of the risks they were taking. I think most of them knew or suspected that if housing prices dropped more than 20 percent on average many banks might go broke, especially because such a big drop in housing prices would herald a recession (regardless of the direct impact on the banking industry), and a recession would increase the default rate even of bank loans unrelated to real estate; it would also further increase mortgage defaults as people lost their jobs.

It is important not to confuse making mistakes

with being stupid. In an op-ed column on February 2, 2009, revealingly entitled "Bailouts for Bunglers," Paul Krugman opposes the claim that the government should not take over banks because it doesn't know how to run them with the argument that the "bunglers" who ran the banks that collapsed last fall don't know how to run banks either. But they do; and if their mistakes should bar them from being permitted to continue to run banks, then the mistakes that Bernanke and Summers and Geithner have made in the regulation of financial intermediation should bar them from managing the nation's economic policy.

Because a great many banks were heavily invested in financing residential real estate, and because banks were financially entangled with one another, if one bank faced a 1 percent probability of failure, then a great many did. Which meant that if the 1 percent probability materialized, so many banks would be broke or nearly broke that the entire system of credit would freeze. And so it happened in September 2008. But no single bank, in the highly competitive financial-intermediation industry, could justify to its shareholders reducing its risk-taking (for example by reducing its leverage), and therefore their return on equity, merely because the risks that it and its competitors were taking might precipitate a financial crisis that could in turn usher in a depression, just as a wave of bank insolvencies caused by the bursting of a credit-fed stock bubble had ushered in the Great Depression of the 1930s and a wave of bank insolvencies caused by the bursting of a real estate bubble had ushered in Japan's "lost decade" of the 1990s. There would be only one effect of the bank's altruism—of its willingness to sacrifice profits enabled by taking a slight risk of bankruptcy that most financial executives would think tolerable, as the risk would be unlikely to materialize for a number of years during which they would be making huge amounts of money: the bank would lose out in competition with its daring competitors. And they *would* be daring, because financial intermediation, being an inherently risky business activity, attracts people who are comfortable with risk.

There was a race to the bottom—or the top, depending on one's perspective. The most daring, aggressive players in the financial sandbox would ramp up the riskiness of their lending or other investing, and this would increase their returns, at least in the short run. Their timid competitors would be forced to match the daring ones' strategy or drop out of the competition. I am told that some bank officials asked the federal regulatory agencies to rein in their competitors, but to no avail.

It is no more realistic to expect banks to internalize the remote risk of economy-wide catastrophe that their lawful pursuit of profit creates than to expect people who fear loss of job and income in a depression to spend, not save, for the greater good, though if enough people save enough money in times of economic trouble, the result could be a disastrous deflation.

What is tolerable risk for a company—that it will very probably go broke sometime during the century—is not for the nation. The risk to the nation is not the bankruptcy of a single major bank but the collapse of the banking industry, precipitating a financial crisis that can bring on a depression— that has done so. This is all the more likely to happen because one of the consequences of easy credit is a high level of personal debt. When a collapse of the banking industry freezes credit, economic output falls because of the disruption of the normal course of business, which depends on credit. With output dropping, layoffs begin. People with heavy debt who lose or fear losing their jobs reduce their spending, which causes a further drop in output. If output falls sharply, as it has been doing in recent months and seems set to continue doing, sellers will reduce their prices in order to retain customers and clear inventory. If the price drop is substantial and creates expectations of further and even deeper price cuts, people may begin hoarding cash, hoping to be able to buy more goods and services in the future because the purchasing power of cash will grow. Hoarding causes further drops in spending and also in borrowing—no one wants to borrow who thinks he'll be repaying the loan in dollars that are worth more because prices will be lower—and then we are in a deflation, and the downward spiral gathers momentum.

Businessmen can no more afford to consider the effect of their decisions on the economy as a whole than consumers can. Consumers spend a smaller part of their incomes in a depression because they want to build up their precautionary savings—but by reducing their spending they make the depression worse. (In the topsy-turvy world of depression economics, it is possible to argue almost with a straight face that people should save when they are flush and spend when they are broke—and that inventory that builds up in a depression should be destroyed to stimulate new production.) Behavior that generates large external costs provides an apt occasion for government regulation.

We are in a depression and struggling to get out of it. But what has brought us to this pass? Low interest rates do not appear from nowhere, nor movements to deregulate the financial sector. The low interest rates of the early 2000s were a product of a deliberate decision by the Federal Reserve. The deregulation movement was the response to justified criticism of common-carrier and public-utility regulation. But the economists who pushed deregulation, as I said, were not macroeconomists sensitive to the role of banking regulation in preventing risk-taking that could bring on a depression, while the macroeconomists viewed low interest rates with complacence because they thought that a depression could easily be prevented, precisely by keeping interest rates low and thus stimulating economic activity. The danger they perceived in low interest rates was inflation, and when the consumer price index stayed down during the early 2000s despite the low interest rates prevailing in that period they thought they had found the Holy Grail. Actually the low interest rates had produced inflationary pressures, but pressures that pushed up the price of housing and to a lesser extent of common stocks rather than the price of items that dominate the consumer price index. Depressions were thought a thing of the past, and Robert Lucas pronounced the end of depression economics and urged macro-economists to shift their attention to issues of economic growth.

Economists were strongly influenced by Milton Friedman's argument that the Great Depression had been the result of the Federal Reserve's shrinking the money supply when prices and output fell in the wake of the stock market crash of October 1929 — that had the Fed kept up the money supply the nation would have experienced nothing worse than a recession. Insufficient weight was given to the fact that the Federal Reserve's creation of money is mediated by the banking industry. The Fed in effect licenses the banks to create money by making loans, and if they are afraid to lend (more precisely, if they set stringent criteria for lending, because the risk of default is so great) and if overindebted people are afraid to borrow lest they have to repay their loans in more valuable dollars, the money supply may shrink despite the Fed's efforts, causing deflation to accelerate as prices fall and firms and individuals hoard cash. At that point, the efforts that the Federal Reserve would have to exert in order to arrest the deflationary spiral might plant the seeds of a terrible post-depression inflation. And in anticipation of the inflation, interest rates might rise rather than fall, choking off recovery from the depression.

The failure of the economics profession to have grasped the dangers that have now produced the first U.S. depression since the 1930s is excusable. Ideology has played a role in this professional blindness, but that is unavoidable because of the difficulty of empirically testing rival theories of depression and the political significance of depressions and responses to them. The fact that finance and macroeconomics have become separate fields with some difficulties of intercommunication may have been the inevitable result of the relentless pressure for ever-greater specialization in academic disciplines. Even the failure of officials and of most academic economists to heed the abundant warning signs of the coming crash is, if not excusable, at least readily understandable; Cassandras rarely receive a fair hearing, and for reasons that only in hindsight can be seen to be mistaken.

What is inexcusable is the failure of the Federal Reserve and other economic agencies within the federal government to have prepared contingency plans for the possibility, remote as it seemed, that a crumbling of the banking industry would set the stage for a depression. When the financial crisis hit in mid-September 2008, the government was unprepared and responded with a series of improvisations that did avert the most catastrophic imaginable consequences of the crisis but could not avert a depression. The improvisations were bumbling, incoherent, poorly explained; the President seemed absent, so far as attending to the economy was concerned, during the critical period. Even now, four and a half months after the crisis hit, the government has no coherent plan of recovery. In the absence of such a plan, it is, or soon will be, trying everything at once—flooding the economy with money, which may not work, as I argued in chapter 5; trying to restore output and employment by massive deficit spending, which may not work either; bailing out the banking industry—or perhaps confiscating much of it ("nationalization") (odd how saving the industry and swallowing it are discussed in the same breath); reforming the regulatory framework and as part of the reform perhaps consolidating the myriad agencies that have a piece of the financial regulatory pie; and relieving mortgagors of some of the burden of their mortgages. All are measures with strengths and weaknesses that cannot be gauged in advance; all suffer from having to be adopted without having been thought out in advance; some, such as regulatory reform, are overly ambitious. And doubtless there is more to come. The atmosphere is electric with proposals for economic recovery—so many that the government may lack the intellectual resources to evaluate them.

I am not a forecaster. I do not know when the recovery from this depression will begin. But if it begins tomorrow, the trillions of dollars that the government has spent to speed recovery, and the restructuring of banking and its reform that will bring in their train untold problems and uncertainties, will overhang the economy for years to come, as when an expensive treatment cures a deadly illness but leaves the patient debilitated.

Further Readings

The following is a list of books and articles that readers of this book may find interesting. The views expressed in them are diverse, and I do not mean by suggesting them to imply that I agree with all of them.

Tobias Adrian and Hyun Song Shin, "Financial Intermediaries, Financial Stability, and Monetary Policy" (forthcoming in *Journal of Economic Perspectives*).

Dean Baker, *Plunder and Blunder: The Rise and Fall of the Bubble Economy* (2009).

Ben S. Bernanke, "Deflation: Making Sure 'It' Doesn't Happen Here," Nov. 21, 2002, www.federalreserve.gov/BOARDDOCS/SPEECHES/2002/20021121/default.htm (visited Jan. 1, 2009).

Olivier Blanchard, "The Crisis: Basic Mechanisms,

and Appropriate Policies" (Dec. 2008), http://
papers.ssrn.com/sol3/papers.cfm?abstract_id=
1324280#.

Markus K. Brunnermeier, "Deciphering the Liquidity and Credit Crunch 2007–08" (forthcoming
in *Journal of Economic Perspectives*).

Richard C. K. Burdekin and Pierre L. Siklos, eds.,
Deflation: Current and Historical Perspectives
(2004).

George Cooper, *The Origin of Financial Crises: Central Banks, Credit Bubbles and the Efficient
Market Failure* (2008).

Brady Dennis and Robert O'Harrow Jr., "A Crack in
the System," *Washington Post*, Dec. 29–31, 2008.

Chris Farrell, *Deflation: What Happens When Prices
Fall* (2004).

Niall Ferguson, *The Ascent of Money: A Financial
History of the World* (2008).

Stanley Fischer and Rudiger Dornbusch, *Introduction to Macroeconomics* (1983).

Irving Fisher, "The Debt-Deflation Theory of Great
Depressions," 1 *Econometrica* 337 (1933).

W. Scott Frame and Lawrence J. White, "Fussing
and Fuming over Fannie and Freddie: How
Much Smoke, How Much Fire?" *Journal of
Economic Perspectives* (Spring 2005): 159.

Peter M. Garber, "Famous First Bubbles," *Journal of Economic Perspectives* (Spring 1990): 35.

James D. Gwartney et al., *Macroeconomics: Private and Public Choice*, pt. 3 (12th ed., 2008).

Takeo Hoshi and Anil K. Kashyap, "Will the U.S. Bank Recapitalization Succeed? Lessons from Japan" (Dec. 2008), http://faculty.chicagogsb.edu/anil.kashyap/research/will_us_bank_recapitalization_succeed2.pdf.

William C. Hunter, George G. Kaufman, and Michael Pamerleano, eds., *Asset Price Bubbles: The Implications for Monetary, Regulatory, and International Policies* (2003).

John Maynard Keynes, *The General Theory of Employment, Interest and Money* (1936).

Charles P. Kindleberger and Robert Z. Aliber, *Manias, Panics, and Crashes: A History of Financial Crises* (5th ed., 2005).

Paul Krugman, *The Return of Depression Economics and the Crisis of 2008* (2008).

Christopher Mayer, Edward Morrison, and Tomasz Piskorski, "A New Proposal for Loan Modifications" (Columbia Business School and Columbia Law School, Jan. 7, 2009).

Randall E. Parker, *The Economics of the Great De-*

pression: A Twenty-First Century Look Back at the Economics of the Interwar Era (2007).

Ľuboš Pástor and Pietro Veronesi, "Was There a NASDAQ Bubble in the Late 1990s?" *Journal of Financial Economics* 81 (2006): 61.

Raghuram G. Rajan, "Has Financial Development Made the World Riskier?" in *The Greenspan Era: Lessons for the Future: A Symposium Sponsored by the Federal Reserve Bank of Kansas City* (2005), 313.

Robert J. Shiller, *The Subprime Solution: How Today's Financial Crisis Happened, and What to Do about It* (2008).

Andrei Shleifer, *Inefficient Markets: An Introduction to Behavioral Finance* (2000).

Mark Zandi, *Financial Shock: A 360° Look at the Subprime Mortgage Implosion, and How to Avoid the Next Financial Crisis* (2008).

Luigi Zingales, "The Future of Securities Regulation" (University of Chicago, Booth Graduate School of Business, Dec. 2008).

Index